D0948352

ELENA KAGAN

ELENA KAGAN

A Biography

Meg Greene

GREENWOOD BIOGRAPHIES

GREENWOOD

AN IMPRINT OF ABC-CLIO, LLC
Santa Barbara, California • Denver, Colorado • Oxford, England

Library of Congress Cataloging-in-Publication Data

Greene, Meg, author.
  Elena Kagan : a biography / Meg Greene.
    pages cm. — (Greenwood biographies)
  Includes index.
  ISBN 978-1-4408-2897-3 (hardback) — ISBN 978-1-4408-2898-0 (ebook)
  1. Kagan, Elena, 1960– 2. United States. Supreme Court—Officials and employees—Biography. 3. Judges—United States—Biography. 4. United States. Solicitor General—Officials and employees—Biography. 5. Government attorneys—United States—Biography. 6. Lawyers—United States—Biography. 7. Law teachers—United States—Biography. I. Title.
  KF8745.K34G74 2014
  347.73'2634—dc23
  [B]   2013031449

ISBN: 978-1-4408-2897-3
EISBN: 978-1-4408-2898-0

18 17 16 15 14   1 2 3 4 5

This book is also available on the World Wide Web as an eBook.
Visit www.abc-clio.com for details.

Greenwood
An Imprint of ABC-CLIO, LLC

ABC-CLIO, LLC
130 Cremona Drive, P.O. Box 1911
Santa Barbara, California 93116-1911

This book is printed on acid-free paper ∞

Manufactured in the United States of America

CONTENTS

SERIES FOREWORD

In response to school and library needs, ABC-CLIO publishes this distinguished series of full-length biographies specifically for student use. Prepared by field experts and professionals, these engaging biographies are tailored for students who need challenging yet accessible biographies. Ideal for school assignments and student research, the length, format, and subject areas are designed to meet educators' requirements and students' interests.

ABC-CLIO offers an extensive selection of biographies spanning all curriculum-related subject areas including social studies, the sciences, literature and the arts, history and politics, and popular culture, covering public figures and famous personalities from all time periods and backgrounds, both historic and contemporary, who have made an impact on American and/or world culture. The subjects of these biographies were chosen based on comprehensive feedback from librarians and educators. Consideration was given to both curriculum relevance and inherent interest. Readers will find a wide array of subject choices from fascinating entertainers like Miley Cyrus and Lady Gaga to inspiring leaders like John F. Kennedy and Nelson Mandela, from the greatest athletes of our time like Michael Jordan and Muhammad Ali to the most amazing success stories of our day like J.K. Rowling and Oprah.

While the emphasis is on fact, not glorification, the books are meant to be fun to read. Each volume provides in-depth information about the subject's life from birth through childhood, the teen years, and adulthood. A thorough account relates family background and education, traces personal and professional influences, and explores struggles, accomplishments, and contributions. A timeline highlights the most significant life events against an historical perspective. Bibliographies supplement the reference value of each volume.

INTRODUCTION

A very astute writer observed that "it's not easy to unring the bell," when it comes to Supreme Court appointments. That is because Supreme Court appointees often far outlast the presidency. Justices, once appointed to the bench of the highest court in the land, often stay for years, if not decades. A presidential library can be a wonderful thing to ensure a legacy of any president, but if one really wants to see something enduring, all it takes is a look at how the Supreme Court votes on any number of issues each year. That is as enduring a presidential legacy if not more so than a library of schedules, mail, and memos.

Under the current administration, now entering into its second term, President Barack Obama has had the opportunity to appoint two new Supreme Court justices to the bench. What this means in the immediate future is that the court may move from its previous position as a conservative court to one that might be called more centrist. What these appointments mean in the long term is anyone's guess.

The court's most junior member—literally—is the former solicitor general of the United States and the dean of Harvard Law School, Elena Kagan. Already at the age of 50, Kagan has broken two glass ceilings—one in academia by becoming the first woman dean of the

Harvard University Law School, and the other in politics by acting as the federal government's top lawyer—with her appointment as solicitor general of the United States. As far back as 2009, Kagan's name was bandied about as a potential Supreme Court justice. The first time, she lost to Sonia Sotomayor, but a year later, it was clear that Kagan's time—and her long-time desire—had finally arrived.

In the three years since her appointment, Kagan has emerged as a bit of a surprise to many who pronounced her early on as too lightweight for the bench. Unlike the majority of justices, Kagan had practiced very little law, and had never held a judgeship—not for lack of trying as her failed attempt to win a seat on the circuit court under the Clinton administration demonstrated. But to judge Kagan on what she does not do—rather than looking at what she has done—first as a clerk to the great legal activist Supreme Court judge Thurgood Marshall, to her academic writings and appointments, to her duties as solicitor general is to seriously underestimate the acumen and diligence Kagan has brought so far to the court.

The Supreme Court is currently experiencing what is known as an extremely "hot bench." That is a polite way of saying the justices ask so many questions at the one-hour session allocated to each case that counsel cannot get a word in. While new justices, in particular, often go silent during their first few weeks and months at the verbal roller derby (the soft-spoken Justice David H. Souter and the mild-mannered Justice Samuel Alito each asked very few questions in their first terms, and Justice Clarence Thomas has not asked a question at oral argument for five years), the two new female justices are different.

In this last term, the three female justices—Ruth Bader Ginsburg, Sonia Sotomayor, and Kagan—dominated the arguments heard by the court. According to one source, Judge Ginsburg was the first to ask a question 37 percent of the time, while Justice Sotomayor asked the most questions—averaging more than 21 queries in an hour-long argument. Where Kagan shines, according to court observers, is not with quantity, but with quality, earning high marks for her "crisp and conversational" questions that often went directly to the heart of a case. And, therein lies Kagan's most promising strength—as an academic with a more intellectual grasp of the law, Kagan can probe a case in ways that other justices do not or cannot.

It is not as if Kagan does not speak—she does. As one observer noted, she is more vocal than her predecessor Justice John Paul Stevens, who was known to sit quietly through most sessions before asking gently if he could ask a question. And unlike Clarence Thomas, who said absolutely nothing in his first two years on the bench, Kagan spoke up during her first time in court, asking 10 questions—and those tended to be brief and concise. And unlike Justice Sonia Sotomayor, who is known to interrupt lawyers and her colleagues during a session to ask a question (in one instance, Chief Justice Roberts stopped Sotomayor as she interrupted Justice Anthony Kennedy and told her to let him finish his question), Kagan waits her turn. But it is a telling difference; as one court observer bluntly stated after one session: "Sotomayor talks. Kagan listens."

Another thing Kagan is not is a zealot. Chalk that up to her experience in representing other institutions, agencies, and groups; but Kagan is already demonstrating that she follows her own course, whatever and wherever the law takes her. She has mastered the ability to keep her own feelings and values out of the way in listening to a case, effectively stopping cold the complaints of those who characterized her as a careerist and self-centered opportunist.

Another surprise has been her talent as a legal writer and she has won kudos for her ability to write readable opinions that anyone can understand, a goal many judges strive for, but few attain. As one reporter who covers the court noted:

> I have been writing about the court the past three terms, and reading her prose has been as enjoyable as watching her in action. No previous justice has written with her emphasis on the vernacular or so matter-of-factly addressed readers as if our views about a case truly mattered.[1]

The report went on to note that Kagan is a master of topic sentence and is not above a dig here and there, although she does it with style. Combined with her insight, her sharp legal analysis and her way with an argument, Kagan may emerge as one of the court's finest writers, an ironic turn of events, in that one of the criticisms that has dogged her throughout the years is scarcity of her legal writings.

As the court's junior member, Kagan was given two specific tasks when she joined the bench. She answers the door when all the justices are in conference and she sits on the Cafeteria Committee. The latter has allowed her to argue for, and win, the bringing of frozen yogurt to the Supreme Court cafeteria. As she told a group at the University of Michigan, "When it comes to the end of my term, if I didn't do anything else, at least I'll be known for that."

Perhaps one of the odder friendships on the court has been between Kagan and Justice Scalia. Almost from the beginning, when Kagan argued her first case as solicitor general, she and Scalia have hit it off. In an interview at George Washington University, Scalia regaled the audience with a recent hunting trip taken with Kagan:

> It was, unfortunately, not successful. . . . We got antelope tags, which are expensive for out of state, and mule deer tags. Didn't get a single shot at an antelope or a mule deer. So she ended up killing a white-tailed doe, which she could have done in my driveway. She dropped that doe with one shot. . . . Boom. Just like that.[2]

Clearly, there is far more to Elena Kagan than many people realize. And court watchers believe that, over time, Kagan may emerge as a significant force on the court, given her mind for the law, her writing, and her willingness to listen.

NOTES

1. Lincoln Caplan, "The Talented Justice Kagan," *New York Times*, June 29, 2013, http://www.nytimes.com/2013/06/30/opinion/sunday/the-talented-justice-kagan.html?ref=kaganelena.

2. Jay Conley, "Antonin Scalia Entertains at Lisner," *George Washington Today*, February 13, 2013, http://gwtoday.gwu.edu/antonin-scalia-entertains-lisner.

TIMELINE: EVENTS IN THE LIFE OF ELENA KAGAN

1960   On April 28, Elena Kagan is born in New York City to Gloria Gittelman Kagan and Robert Kagan.

1977   Graduates from Hunter College High School in New York City.

1981   Graduates with honors from Princeton University with a BA in history.

1983   Receives a master's degree in philosophy from Worcester College at Oxford University.

1986   Graduates with honors from Harvard Law School.

1986–1987   Clerks for Judge Abner Mikva at the U.S. Court of Appeals for the District of Columbia Circuit.

1987–1988   Serves as law clerk to Supreme Court Justice Thurgood Marshall.

1989–1991   Enters private practice at the Washington, D.C., law firm Williams & Connolly.

1991–1995   Teaches at the University of Chicago Law School.

1993   Spends summer working with Senator Joseph Biden on Judiciary Committee; meets Barack Obama.

1994   Kagan's father, Robert Kagan, dies at age 67.

1995   Earns tenure at the University of Chicago Law School.

1995–1996 Works as associate counsel to President Bill Clinton.

1997–1999 Deputy assistant to President Clinton for domestic policy and deputy director of the Domestic Policy Council.

1999   President Clinton nominates Kagan to the U.S. Court of Appeals for the District of Columbia Circuit, but Republicans controlling the Senate never act on the nomination.

1999–2001 Visiting professor, Harvard Law School.

2001   Works as professor at Harvard Law School.

2003–2009 Appointed first female dean of Harvard Law School.

2004   Campus recruitment controversy over "Don't Ask, Don't Tell" policy.

2007   Named as outside advisor by New York governor Eliot Spitzer to commission on education; overhauls curriculum at Harvard.

2008   Kagan's mother, Gloria Gittelman Kagan, dies.

2009   By a 61–31 vote, the Senate confirms Kagan as the nation's first female solicitor general; joins Supreme Court bar, so she can argue cases in front of that court; argues first case in front of the Supreme Court.

2010   On May 10, Kagan is nominated to the Supreme Court by President Barack Obama; on August 5, Kagan is confirmed, becoming the fourth woman to ascend to the nation's highest court.

Chapter 1

THE STREETS OF NEW YORK

Bounded by 58th Street to the south, Central Park to the east, and the Hudson River to the west lies one of New York City's most famous neighborhoods: the Upper West Side. The northern boundary of the neighborhood is less evident. Historically, the neighborhood is considered to end at 110th Street near Central Park, but more modern sensibilities place it at 125th Street which includes the neighborhood of Morningside Heights. The backbone of the neighborhood is considered to be the diagonally angled 66-block stretch of Broadway, which intersects with Columbus Circle, Lincoln Square, and Straus Park.

The neighborhood is home to some of the nation's—and the world's—priciest real estate, with coveted addresses to be found along Riverside Drive, West End Avenue, Columbus Avenue, and, long considered the jewel in the crown, Central Park West. Here are found some of the most famous residences in the world, including apartment buildings such as the Dakota, the San Remo, the El Dorado, the Century, 15 Central Park West, and the Majestic. The area is a pleasing mixture of old and new architecture that, instead of clashing, complement each other in such a way that merely emphasizes the area's urban gentility.

The Upper West Side is also home to a number of famous city land-marks, including the Cathedral of Saint John the Divine, Union Theo-logical Seminary, the Jewish Theological Seminary of America, and Riverside Church. Educational institutions are numerous too, with some of the more famous being Columbia University and Barnard Col-lege. Cultural institutions, such as the Lincoln Center, made its home in the Upper West Side as has the vital hub of commerce—the Time Warner Center. And one of the city's more popular tourist attractions, Grant's Tomb, is found in the neighborhood, located in Central Park.

THE STORY OF A NEIGHBORHOOD

The story of the Upper West Side begins in the early 17th century when the area was first settled by Dutch immigrants. The settlement became known as Bloemendal, or "Valley of Flowers," and consisted mostly of small farms and villages. By the 18th century, the area was known for its tobacco as well as a thriving center of commerce, so much so, that a special road known as Bloomingdale Road was built in 1703 to handle the traffic. This road later became Broadway. By the late 18th century, the area was home to a number of wealthy Dutch merchants who had built large country estates.[1]

Well into the 19th century, the Upper West Side continued to be a bastion of relatively isolated wealthy estates and mansions with sev-eral small villages. However, in 1853, with the construction of Central Park, many of the area's poorer residents were displaced. This large-scale removal of the poor and less desirable elements impacted the West Side tremendously. Where once the area was known for its picturesque villages and imposing mansions, there now appeared small and poorly constructed lean-tos and shanties. By 1865, a growing population finally forced the once bucolic suburb of Bloemendal to become part of New York City. Still, the area, compared to other thriving neighborhoods in the city, remained largely undeveloped well into the late 19th century.[2]

The Upper West Side's character underwent a more dramatic change with the development of the area in the late 19th century, as real estate developers began the construction of several large apartment buildings, including the Dakota (completed in 1884). This expansion continued well into the 20th century, and over time, other shops and businesses followed. Each street and avenue also cultivated its own atmosphere: for low-rent housing and small family owned shops: Amsterdam Avenue was the place cheap housing and shops, Columbus Avenue became a thriving center of commerce; Riverside Drive soon became known as a street filled with homes, both grand and humble. With the opening of the city subway system in 1904, the West End enjoyed even better access to the rest of the city. In turn, city residents now began to settle and to work in the area in greater numbers.[3]

THE MELTING POT AND THE UPPER WEST SIDE

Adding to the neighborhood's growing cultural and artistic life during the late 19th century was the relocation of Columbia University, one of the nation's first colleges. The school moved from its East Side location to the neighborhood of Morningside Heights, on the grounds of the former Bloomingdale Lunatic Asylum. The school's new location soon drew students, teachers, and other intellectuals and artists to make their homes in the Upper West Side. Barnard College, established in 1889 and located in Morningside Heights near Columbia, also reinforced the area's growing reputation as a center for the city's intellectual elite.

The neighborhood was a true melting pot. People from all over the world came to the Upper West Side, including African Americans from the South, immigrants from Russia, Poland, and the Ukraine, as well as people from the Dominican Republic, Haiti, and Puerto Rico. Jews made up one of the more prevalent groups living and working in the Upper West Side, having first arrived in New York City from Russia and Poland beginning in the late 19th century. The influx continued well into World War II, as Jewish refugees seeking asylum from Hitler's Germany made their way to New York City and the Upper West Side. Beginning in the years after World War II, a growing number of homosexuals also made their way to the neighborhood, setting off a wave of gentrification of the area's older buildings.[4]

Beginning in the 1960s, the Upper West Side underwent a change in character marked by an increase in tenement housing and a growing reputation as a rough and undesirable neighborhood; the seedy facades of several buildings later provided the exterior shots for the popular movie musical about warring gangs in the West Side, *West Side Story*. By the 1980s, the Upper West Side's popularity and social attractiveness had diminished even further due to crime, though the community still attracted artists, writers, and young families, drawn by the neighborhood's eclectic feel and low rents.[5]

The ever-changing character of the Upper West Side has kept the neighborhood diverse as well as more liberal in its political and social attitudes. This resulted in a community where many different kinds of people come together. This was especially true beginning in the 1950s, when the construction of the Lincoln Center was getting underway. When it was revealed that several families living in slum housing would be displaced to make way for the new cultural center, debates over the methods and plan for the Lincoln Center drew many members together in protest.[6]

It would be amidst this center of diverse and ever-changing swirl of energy of the Upper West Side that a New York attorney, Robert Kagan, would move with his small family to make a home and life. It was also where Kagan's only daughter, Elena Kagan, would cut her teeth on the politics of diversity.

Supreme Court Justice Elena Kagan lights a menorah before speaking at the 6th & I Historic Synagogue in Washington, D.C. (AP Photo/Alex Brandon)

MEET THE KAGANS

Sometime after World War II, a young man by the name of Robert Kagan was traveling on a crowded train in Pennsylvania. He was a student at Penn State University (the first in his family to go to college), and was on his way home to spend the holidays with family in Flatbush, Brooklyn. The son of Ukranian Jewish immigrants, Kagan's father manufactured and sold hats and clothing. After graduating from high school, Kagan served during World War II as a sergeant in the U.S. Army. Once the war ended, he decided to pursue his education at Penn State.

Spotting a young woman standing in the train Robert Kagan offered his seat and the two struck up a conversation. Her name was Gloria Gittelman, and she also was headed home for the holidays to South Philadelphia. Like Kagan, she was the first in her family to go to college. The two soon began dating. After Robert Kagan's graduation from Penn State in 1948, he applied and was accepted to Yale Law School, where he graduated in 1951. In between, he found time to marry Gloria Gittelman in 1950.[7]

Gloria Gittelman was also the child of Jewish immigrants who had settled in Philadelphia from Poland. Her father owned a dairy business on South Seventh Street, and the family, which included her father Laizar, her mother Esther, and her brother Stanley, lived above the store on the building's two upper floors. Gloria's mother worked at the counter serving customers, while her father drove a truck making deliveries of eggs, butter, and cheese to local luncheonettes and markets throughout the city. As a young girl who had just learned to count, Gloria, along with her brother, were regular fixtures at the store counter helping with customers and other chores.[8]

Even as a young girl, Gloria displayed a keen and fierce intellect which eventually got her into the noted girl's school, the Philadelphia High School for Girls, one of the most competitive and well-regarded schools in the city. Established in 1848, the school was one of the first public schools for women established in the nation. The school's motto, *Vincit qui se vincit* ("she conquers who conquers herself"), seemed especially apt, given the general attitudes of the time toward women who sought higher education and the opportunities it might bring. As a student,

Gloria Gittelman distinguished herself and at the age of 16 graduated from the school. She then went on to Penn State to continue her studies with the goal of becoming a teacher.[9]

THE HEART OF A TEACHER

After the couple married, they moved first to the New York City neighborhood of Bensonhurst. Eventually, Gloria found a job teaching students at a school in Harlem, and then later secured a job teaching at the Hunter College Elementary School, an institution not unlike the Philadelphia High School for Girls. For those who knew her, including family, friends, and students, the power of education was Gloria Kagan's mantra throughout her life. Teaching fifth and sixth grade students, Kagan was at once encouraging yet demanding, which often left more than one child in tears. As one former student explained, "She was a teacher who just gave so much of herself, and she expected that in return from everyone, all the time. . . . For the student who really rises to that expectation, it's great. But for the student who might be a little more creative or messy, I think it was really hard." These high expectations, on more than one occasion, led Gloria Kagan into yelling and shouting matches with her students.[10]

Another student remembered Kagan as a "teacher we should all have once in our lives . . . someone who makes a student out of you, who makes you go the extra mile." Still another student remembered how Kagan would immerse her students in whatever subject was at hand. In 1976, the year of the American Bicentennial, students in Mrs. Kagan's class learned all about the American Revolution by studying the art of the period, memorizing the poem "Paul Revere's Ride," and taking a field trip to Philadelphia to visit the Liberty Bell and Constitution Hall. "We studied the bicentennial the way medical students study the kidney—from every direction," the student recalled. "Her value system was to learn something: don't fritter away your time being 12."[11]

Still, Kagan's outbursts in class did not go unnoticed; on more than one occasion, the principal would have to speak to her. Stanley Seidman, a former principal at the school, remembers speaking to Mrs. Kagan stating, "I did talk to her about calming down and told her that they are still children and have a ways to go. . . . In almost all cases, it wasn't anger that was vicious. It was more her being upset with the students for not wanting to push themselves a step further."[12]

WORKING THE LAW

In the meantime, Robert Kagan was busy trying to establish himself. He first found employment with firms specializing in corporate and tax law, and for the next several years established himself as a solid lawyer with a thorough knowledge of tax and business law. Finally, in 1973, Kagan decided to go into practice with an old childhood friend, Bill J. Lubic; both men had attended Lafayette High School in Bensonhurst, Brooklyn. Lubic, like the Kagans, also lived in Stuyvesant Town, a large and private residential development located on the East Side in Manhattan. The development, which completed construction in 1947, was considered one of the most iconic and successful private housing communities built after World War II. The complex spread over 80 acres and included red brick apartment buildings, playgrounds, and a park. The development would grow to include over 8,700 apartments in 35 residential buildings. Along with its neighboring development, the Peter Cooper Village, the area was home to over 25,000 persons.[13]

By this time, both men had been practicing law for almost two decades. With Lubic's extensive legal experience in management and real estate coupled with Kagan's corporate law and tax background, the two men seemed ideally suited to forge a partnership that would mean taking on the deep and murky waters that made up New York City's real estate world. Both men also believed strongly in community activism, and so focused on legal issues dealing with co-op/condo legal representation. The pair would soon become well known for their work and leadership role in the community; in time, the partnership would evolve into one of the most active and influential legal firms in New York.[14]

Kagan and Lubic's practice centered on the representation of tenants affected by co-op conversions, which by the 1970s was sweeping through the city. This practice, which entailed the turning around of apartment building rentals to be sold as individual condo or co-op units, was not without controversy. For tenants, particularly those of little means, a co-op conversion often meant they could no longer afford to live in the building. Kagan and Lubic focused their practice on working with tenants to help them navigate the process and protect the tenants' legal rights from unscrupulous realtors or building owners. "We represented about 300 tenant groups who were fearful of leaving their homes, suspicious of the bait being offered and angry at being forced into a co-oping process few of them knew anything about," said Lubic in 1994. "Bob was inventive, skillful, a tough negotiator and an effective advocate. . . . But always [he] had the human touch—the touch of a man who loved and respected his fellow human beings."[15]

One of the first co-op conversions the two men took on was located at 320 West End Avenue, where Kagan had recently moved his family to what was known as a "classic 6," consisting of a living room, formal dining room, two bedrooms, two baths, and a maid's room and bath. The building's owner had gone into default. As Lubic later recalled, "Bob and I had an office on Avenue of the Americas at 47th Street, a half block away from the bank's office, and we walked in there [to the bank] and said, 'Don't you want to get rid of this?'" The two lawyers ended up working with many of the building's three dozen or so tenants to aid them in buying their apartments. The men's work extended long past regular business hours. Lubic remembers that working with tenant groups often meant meetings in the evenings and weekends. He also describes his friend and law partner as one who was "really committed to the law, not to the financial monuments but to the principle, and using it to help people."[16]

COMMUNITY ACTIVISM

Kagan's community activism extended well beyond his law office. During the 1970s, he served as chairman of both Community Board 7 and Combo, a committee of West Side neighborhood groups who were protesting a construction project known as Westway. The project proposed to extend the western shore of Manhattan with landfill, while burying a new highway underneath a park as well as creating a new commercial and residential development. Kagan and the groups protested against the project stating it would create more traffic while further degrading the environment; in particular the groups were concerned on the possible impact on striped bass fish that resided in the Hudson River. One member of an environmental group who worked with Kagan stated that "He encouraged the kind of honest public debate over major policy issues that is sadly lacking today." The project in the end was defeated. However, there was a bit of irony to be had. The architect of Westway, Craig Whitaker, remembered one meeting with Mr. Kagan in which Kagan gave a very spirited discussion on the evils of private car ownership in New York City. Whitaker then remembered that as soon as the meeting was over, Kagan left the building and hopped into a friend's car. Whitaker never let the lawyer forget it.[17]

Kagan was also known to engage in a bit of theater if the situation called for it. A member of Community Board 7, which acted as a kind of liaison between the city and residents of the neighborhood, remembered receiving a call from Robert Kagan very early one morning. Workers were getting ready to cut down several trees in Riverside Park and Kagan wanted to stop them. Kagan told his friend, "Get over here and bring a rope." But the friend only had a jump rope. She took it to Kagan who, wrapping the rope around himself, his friend, and a tree, told the workers, "You have no plan and no permits and you can't take these trees down." In the end, only two trees were taken down, but Kagan had made his point.[18]

Kagan also found time to serve as president of the United Parents Association, a citywide advocacy group that consisted of parent groups affiliated with public schools throughout the city. He also served as a trustee of the West End Synagogue. His partner Bill Lubic later stated that Kagan "was one of these people whom everyone liked and everyone believed. . . . He could deal with people in extremely difficult circumstances—everything at the grass-roots level on the Upper West Side was a major problem. That was his talent. I firmly believe that that's what his daughter got from their relationship."[19]

THE OTHER SIDE

However, not everyone saw Robert Kagan as a champion of the people. In a series of articles written for the community paper *Heights and Valley News* beginning in July 1981, Kagan was accused of a major conflict of interest in representing tenants of a building located at 300 West 108th Street. According to the article, Kagan stood to make a handsome profit from the building's conversion to co-op apartments, and not just from assisting tenants in buying their apartments, but also as a partner in a business offering to buy apartments from tenants who could not afford to stay.[20]

The partnership, known as Apartment Investors Associates, sent letters to the tenants offering to buy tenants' apartments if the conversion went through. This was a common enough practice during co-op conversions, allowing speculators to advance money to tenants who would otherwise be unable to purchase their apartments. The price was usually close to the lower insider price being offered to people who lived in the building. Then, after the conversion, tenants would sell the apartment to the speculators, who in turn would sell the apartment at a much higher price on the open market. According to the article, tenants interested were asked to contact the company and then negotiations would begin.[21]

At the time of the building's conversion, Kagan had signed a contract with one tenant who was considered to be the primary advocate for the conversion in the building. In addition to Kagan's $12,000 fee and the provision that he would become the lawyer for the co-op if the conversion succeeded, he would also earn an additional $4,500–$6,000 for the building's successful co-op conversion. Part of the problem was that none of the other tenants were aware of either the contract or the stipulation of the extra monies that Kagan would earn. With Kagan's partnership with Apartment Investors Associates, he stood to earn even more money with the sale of any unit in the building.[22]

The accusations against Kagan steamrolled into an investigation by the State Attorney General's Office by October 1981, on charges of possible conflicts of interest with co-op speculation and representation of tenants. The Attorney General's Office was particularly interested in a document filed by Kagan known as a CPS.3, which states that an attorney cannot collect more than $250 from each tenant participating in a tenant co-op plan. In the case of the West End building named in the document, Kagan had collected $4,500 from each tenant. Even though there is a provision allowing an exemption to the $250 limit, it was determined that Kagan had never filed for an exemption. In the end, Kagan paid a $2,000 fine for excess collections. But the consequences of his actions soon led to his dismissal by several tenant associations who had considered hiring him to handle their co-op conversions, as well as being fired by a tenant group that had just hired him. In addition, Kagan was asked to step down from his seat as chair of the ethics committee of Community Board 7. He never served on the board again.[23]

In spite of Kagan's troubles with the state, he continued to thrive in his law practice and other community activities. His wife, firmly committed to her teaching and to providing the best opportunities for learning that she could, also added energy and vitality to their partnership. It would be this heady combination of politics, idealism, and activism, combined with the entertaining and pulsating political scene that was New York in the 1970s that would serve as the backdrop for their three children. The heady combination would affect each child, but particularly the daughter in ways no one could possibly have foreseen.

NOTES

1. Sarah Waxman, "The History of the Upper West Side," n.d., http://www.ny.com/articles/upperwest.html.

2. Ibid.

3. Ibid.

4. Ibid.

5. Ibid.

6. Ibid.

7. Lisa Foderaro and Christine Haughney, "The Kagan Family: Left-Leaning and Outspoken," New York Times, June 18, 2010, p. MB1.

8. Ibid.

9. Ibid.; "Philadelphia High School for Girls," http://webgui.phila.k12.pa.us/schools/g/girlshigh.

10. Foderaro and Haughney, "The Kagan Family."

11. Ibid.

12. Ibid.

13. "Stuyvesant Town History," n.d., http://www.chpcny.org/2010/02/stuyvesant-town-history/.

14. Kagan, Lupic, Lepper Finklestein & Gold: Attorneys at Law, http://www.kll-law.com/bio-wlubic.asp.

15. Michael Daly, "Educated in School —& On City's Streets," *Daily News*, May 11, 2012, p. 6.

16. Foderaro and Haughney, "The Kagan Family."

17. Ibid.

18. Ibid.

19. Obituary, "Robert Kagan 67, Lawyer for Tenants," *New York Times*, July 25, 1994, http://www.nytimes.com/1994/07/25/obituaries/robert-kagan-67-lawyer-for-tenants.html; Sheryl Gay Stolberg, Katharine Q. Seelye, and Lisa W. Foderaro, "A Climb Marked by Confidence and Canniness," *New York Times*, May 10, 2012, http://www.nytimes.com/2010/05/10/us/politics/10kagan.html?pagewanted=5&_r=0.

20. Andre Smith, "Tenants' Lawyer Kagan Found Banking on Co-op Success," *Heights and Valley News*, July–August 1981, pp. 1, 11.

21. Ibid., p. 11.

22. Ibid., pp. 1, 11.

23. Andre Smith, "Kagan to Pay $2000 for Excess Collections: Fired by Tenants for Co-op Speculation," *Heights and Valley News*, October, 1981, p. 4.

Chapter 2

GROWING UP

In the midst of establishing a law practice for Robert and Gloria's teaching, the Kagans found time to start a family. By this time, the Kagans were living in a four-room apartment in Stuyvesant Town, a large private residential development located in east Manhattan. The first child, a boy, Marc, arrived in 1957, followed by their only daughter Elena, born on April 28, 1960. A third child and second son, Irving, followed in 1965. Unlike her tough demeanor at school, Gloria Kagan apparently shifted gears once she got home. A neighbor recalled her as being much more playful with her own children. Her former neighbor also added that it probably helped that all three of the Kagan children were quite driven, so Gloria did not need to nag at them like she might her students.

The three Kagan children came of age during one of the most contentious periods in American history: the 1970s. The decade was filled with social unrest and change that touched almost every level of American society. Building on the civil rights and antiwar movements of the 1960s, many different groups representing a multitude of diverse peoples, creeds, and philosophies created a colorful mosaic of revolutionary social change.

DARK DAYS

New York City during the 1970s might still have appeared to be a mecca for all that was sophisticated and urban; but the reality was quite different. The period is regarded by many native New Yorkers as the city's nadir. On one hand, the city was still a popular tourist attraction, as well as being home to the nation's financial district. On the other hand, the city was plagued by high crime, a deteriorating infrastructure, and political and social unrest.

The city's subway system was deemed unsafe because of crime and was the subject of frequent breakdowns. Policemen accompanied by police dogs rode the subways in an attempt to thwart criminals. City parks were filled with litter and dirt, and people were accosted by panhandlers. In the evenings, muggers and rapists trolled through the parks, looking for potential victims. Times Square had been taken over by prostitutes, drug dealers, and the homeless. Burned out and abandoned buildings dotted the city landscape. Even the New York City Police Department was not immune as investigations into widespread corruption within that institution became pervasive.

The city was also struggling financially. Trading on the New York Stock Exchange declined, while welfare spending continued to escalate. In an attempt to try and stretch funds, the city cut back on a number of services; these cutbacks were especially hard on the poorer neighborhoods. At one point, the city was on the brink of bankruptcy, but was saved at the last minute by a large federal loan. Certainly one of the most notorious events concerning the city's financial life came in October 1975 when then-mayor Abraham Beame requested that the teacher's union invest $150 million from its pension fund to city securities. At the 11th hour, the teacher's union president allowed for the funds to be released and used. Still, the city was foundering. It did not help that less than two weeks later after this event, President Gerald refused to help the city out. His decision was famously summarized by the *New York Daily News* headline "Ford to City: Drop Dead." Ford later backed off, allowing federal loans to the beleaguered city.[1]

As if that was not enough to contend with, the city also experienced a major blackout in July 1977. The ordeal plunged the entire city into darkness for 25 hours. During that time, a number of African

American and Hispanic neighborhoods were looted and subject to other acts of violence. Over 1,000 fires had been set with an additional 1,700 false alarms called in to the city fire departments. By the time the power was restored, over 3,000 people had been arrested. The city was also being terrorized by the Son of Sam serial killer, who appeared to be randomly picking victims and shooting them. For many city residents, the city's problems had become too much; by the end of the decade more than one million people had fled New York City, opting for the quieter suburbs or smaller towns of the state. Clearly, between the crime, the financial crisis, and the damage from the blackouts, many city residents as well as other Americans believed that New York City would never recover.[2]

LIFE IN THE WEST END

By the time Elena was in her teens, the Kagans had moved to the Upper West Side. The neighborhood that Robert and Gloria Kagan raised their children in was one of New York City's most diverse with a colorful history. Unlike several of the tonier neighborhoods and upper middle class enclaves which were primarily white and Protestant, the Upper West End boasted one of the more diverse populations in the city. According to a study conducted in 1966, out of the 150,000 people who made the neighborhood their home, 105,000 were white, 26,000 were Hispanic, and 18,000 residents were African American. There was a relatively large Jewish population in the neighborhood too: of the 105,000 whites who lived in the neighborhood, 40,000 or roughly more than one-third were Jewish. As one journalist wrote at the time, "Only in Honolulu, is there a greater confusion of blood, ancestry, language, and culture in as small a space."[3]

The Jewish families, like the Kagans, who made their home in the Upper West Side were characterized as primarily secular, though the Kagans were active in a local synagogue. However, it appears they were unusual. During the time of their residence, three conservative synagogues located in a 15-block radius from 100th Street to 86th Street had fallen into disrepair as they were used so little. The neighborhood's few Orthodox residents tended to keep to themselves, worshipping quietly.[4]

This melting pot of cultures did not mean that the neighborhood residents were all accepting of each other. In fact, there were often present racial and ethnic tensions between the different groups. But as writer Jon Podhoretz, a journalist and former resident of the neighborhood, pointed out, the tensions stemmed more from class than anything else. Podhoretz also noted that even within each class there were divisions, all of which could lead to highly contentious relations among neighbors. The dominant groups in the neighborhood were the middle class, which consisted of a diverse group of working professionals, academics, teachers, union officials, and social workers. There were the working poor, who held union jobs or who worked at some type of unskilled labor. Then there was a growing welfare class, marked by individuals who did not work at all but depended on state or federal assistance. Still, the neighborhood area boasted a vitality and exuberance about it that would have fit well with the growing Kagan family.[5]

A GROWING SOCIAL AWARENESS

The 1970s also saw New York City as a hotbed of social activism, which no doubt contributed to lively conversations in the Kagan household. In spite of the ongoing problems of crime, waste, and financial problems, the city was also home to a number of groups firmly committed to change. The focus of these groups ranged from preserving the city's architectural landmarks to a new attention on civil rights of different communities.

During the 1960s, one of the most pressing concerns for many city residents was the rapidly disappearing built landscape of the city. With the demolition of the old Pennsylvania Railway Station, as well as the seemingly ongoing destruction of other city landmarks, several citizens banded together to form one of the earliest historic preservation groups in the nation. By the 1970s, the group was a vital force in city politics and city planning. As a result, New York City tried harder to strike a balance between the old and the new, and in the process protect its treasured architectural heritage. In addition, with the help of the historic preservation groups, several neighborhoods, such as SoHo, Tribeca, and Greenwich Village, bounced back from empty, decaying streets of neglected buildings to thriving centers of commerce and residential life.

Perhaps, one of the more dramatic events in American social and cultural history came with the Stonewall Riots in 1969. In the early morning hours of Saturday, June 28, a number of NYPD police officers from the Public Morals Squad raided the popular gay bar, the Stonewall Inn, in Greenwich Village. The raid set off several days of demonstrations and clashes with the police. The event also sparked the first gay pride march in the country, as hundreds of gay men and women walked from Washington Square Park to Central Park. The Stonewall Riots gave birth to the modern gay rights movements, which soon emerged as one of the most cohesive and potent political and social forces in the country.[6]

Other minority groups, including African Americans and Hispanics, also were hard at work in the city during the late 1960s and early 1970s. For blacks and Hispanics, there was a growing awareness of the disparity in education, job, housing, and other opportunities in their communities. Utilizing local churches and other activist organizations, these groups lobbied for improved schools, better job training, and opportunities, as well as continuing to hammer away at the institutional and cultural racism facing them in American society.

A WOMAN IN THE HOUSE

In the midst of the social upheaval and turmoil in the city, there appeared a new political force too; one that signaled more change not just in New York, but nationwide. In 1970, 50-year-old Bella Azbug, an attorney, noted grassroots activist and a noted reform Democrat, was urged to run for Congress. With her flamboyant hats and off-the-cuff remarks, Azbug symbolized the changing fortunes of political life. She won the election as the first woman running on a women's rights and peace platform. She served as a representative of the neighborhoods, including Little Italy, the Lower East Side, and the West Side where the Kagans lived. As Azbug famously proclaimed during her campaign, "This woman's place is in the House-the House of Representatives." In the aftermath of her victory, her daughter added, "We got her out of our house and into your House."[7]

U.S. Representative Bella Azbug.
(Library of Congress)

Azbug's legacies to her constituents and other Americans were her amazing achievements in the area of women's rights. A tireless organizer, Azbug helped create the National Women's Political Caucus as well as serving as head strategist for the Democratic Women's Committee, which worked vigorously to achieve equal representation for women in all elective and appointed posts. She initiated the congressional caucus on women's issues and wrote the first law that banned discrimination against women in obtaining credit, credit cards, loans, and mortgages. Among her other pioneering efforts was the introduction of Congressional bills that focused on comprehensive child care, Social Security for homemakers, family planning, and abortion rights. In 1975, she again broke new ground with the introduction of an amendment to the Civil Rights Act that protected the rights of gays and lesbians.[8]

This was the world that the Kagan children grew up in; and each child would be imprinted in some way by the events of the period.

GROWING UP

Because of Elena Kagan's reluctance to talk of her childhood and early life, there is not a lot of information about her formative years.

The family resided in a third floor apartment at West End Avenue and 75th Street that was comfortable but not fancy. Kagan would share a bedroom with her two brothers. The home was filled with books and art, as well as friends and neighbors who dropped in to share meals and spirited discussions over the events of the day. As one relative later stated, "They [the Kagans] were people who had a very keen sense of social justice." Another cousin remembered that "Verbal sparring was commonplace in their home. . . . They just really enjoyed debating and discussing everything." Many evenings were spent around the dinner table discussing events at the local, national, and international levels. Discussion was encouraged as were questions in the Kagan household. By the time she reached adolescence, Kagan was becoming her father's daughter: fearless, thoughtful, and a mediator when necessary.[9]

The *Bat Mitzvah*

Already, as a young girl, Elena Kagan was proving to be a star student. This was especially evident in her Hebrew school classes at the Conservative Lincoln Square Synagogue. The synagogue, located at 200 Amsterdam Avenue, was noted not only for its unusual round design, but also for its introduction of adult education programs as well as holding lectures on subjects, such as Jewish history, sexuality, and the afterlife. The synagogue held fast to tradition, such as the *mechitza*, which is the physical partition that separates the men and women during services; but the congregation was also noted as being more egalitarian than other synagogue communities. Lincoln Square soon developed a reputation for introducing Jewish families to a more modern brand of Orthodoxy, which many younger Jews found appealing. The Kagan family attended services on occasion, but all the children were made to attend Hebrew School, in which Jewish children learn about the history, culture, and language of Judaism. It also helped that the synagogue was overseen by an energetic and forward thinking young rabbi.[10]

At the age of 13, Elena Kagan wanted to mark her coming-of-age with a special ceremony for young Jewish girls know as a *bat mitzvah*. This ceremony, according to Jewish tradition, recognizes young women as coming of age and now ready to enjoy the same rights as adults. In other words, it marked the beginning of a new life in that the young woman was now morally and ethically responsible for her actions and decisions.

The *bat mitzvah* is a relatively young tradition, at least by Jewish standards. For centuries, Jewish women were prohibited from participating directly in their religious services. However, by the late 19th and early 20th centuries, some Jewish congregations began experimenting with a ceremony, similar in nature to that of the *bar mitzvah*, the coming-of-age ceremony held for young Jewish boys. In 1922, the first *bat mitzvah* was held in the United States. Rabbi Mordecai Kaplan performed a ceremony for his daughter Judith, in which she was allowed to read from the Torah, the Jewish books of scripture. Kaplan's ceremony became the model for the gradual evolution of the *bat mitzvah* ceremony in the United States.[11]

With at least some precedent behind her, Kagan asked for the ceremony to be performed at the Lincoln Synagogue. The problem was Rabbi Riskin had never done one. It did not help the situation either that Kagan had strong opinions about what she wanted, which did not agree with the rabbi's ideas. But the two negotiated and, finally, with the help of her maternal grandfather in Philadelphia, who convinced the rabbi that girls deserved the opportunity for their own coming-of-age ceremonies, a resolution was worked out.

In a later interview, Rabbi Riskin recalled that "Elena Kagan felt very strongly that there should be [a] ritual bat mitzvah in the synagogue, no less important than the ritual bar mitzvah. . . . This was really the first formal bat mitzvah we had." However, when Kagan asked to read from the Torah on a Saturday morning, the traditional day that *bar mitzvah* ceremonies are held, she was told she could not. Instead, her ceremony would be held on a Friday evening, where she would read from the Book of Ruth; in addition, she would be allowed to speak on her reading during the ceremony.[12]

Kagan's request was not unusual in the larger sphere of women and their changing roles in Judaism. By the early 1970s, feminism had entered the synagogue; in 1972, a group of Conservative Jewish women founded Ezrat Nashim, loosely translated as women's section or women's help. One of the group's first efforts was in petitioning Conservative leaders for equality. One of these areas was the *bat mitzvah*, in which girls were allowed to read from the Torah. Already, in Reform and Reconstructionist synagogues this practice had been established. A scholar of Jewish history commented that:

> In terms of timing, this was the period when young women coming of age, who had those kinds of expectations for equality and taking leadership positions in the secular world, began to question: "Why can't I do this in the Jewish world?" What is unusual is that she [Kagan] asked it in an Orthodox institution where that was an unheard-of question at that point.[13]

In retrospect, Rabbi Riskin admitted that even though they created what he believed was a lovely service, he also realized that Kagan was not entirely satisfied with the ceremony. Riskin also admitted that Kagan's efforts "certainly raised my consciousness." Since then, *bat mitzvahs* at Lincoln Square have evolved to the point where a girl can choose to not only read from the Torah but can lead the ceremony, as long as the service is held in a synagogue annex. There cannot be more than nine men in attendance and they must sit behind the *mechitza*. Girls also have the option of celebrating in the main synagogue after Saturday service, but they cannot read from the Torah.[14]

Kagan's ceremony was memorable for another reason: she ended up consoling a 13-year-old boy whose reception for his *bar mitzvah* was taking place with her own celebration. The boy's parents were divorcing and his grandmothers were fighting over where the boy would sit. A cantor who instructed Kagan for her *bat mitzvah* recalled that "Elena went over to him and asked him to sit down and comforted him and showed him a great deal of compassion and concern."[15]

HUNTER COLLEGE HIGH SCHOOL

Kagan's teenage years were spent attending Hunter College High School where her mother still taught classes. The school was located in an office building at 46th Street and Lexington Avenue where it operated on three floors. Hunter College High School was also unusual among New York City's public schools in that the institution is publicly financed and managed but not run by the city's Department of Education. The school, which went coed soon after Kagan

graduated in 1977, promoted itself as a rigorous learning institution
that also provides nurturing and guidance. It also stressed the importance of public service, an ideal that Kagan was already familiar with,
given her parents, particularly her father's activities, both in and out
of his legal office.

The school, which holds classes from kindergarten to the 12th grade,
was highly competitive. For instance, to win one of the coveted
50 slots for kindergarten, the child must take an I.Q. test and participate in a class observation. High school begins in seventh grade instead
of the traditional ninth grade. The school had a reputation as one of
the city's most elite learning institutions for high school girls; because
of its reputation, it attracted students from all over the city and from
a wide variety of backgrounds. Cram schools were created to help students have a shot at entering the institution through its competitive
combined math, reading, and essay tests required for admission. "There
was no driver's ed, there was no home economics, you didn't learn to
type," said a graduate and classmate of Kagan's. "You were reading great
books, and you were going to college. You were going to lead, you were
going to give back."[16]

Money had little influence at Hunter—students were admitted on
the basis of their performance on the entrance exam rather than family,
social, political, or money connections. One former student remembered that:

> We were really exposed to tremendous diversity there—whether
> it was a Jewish girl from the Upper West Side or a cop's kid from
> the Bronx or the daughter of a C.E.O. from the Upper East Side
> or kids whose parents worked in sweatshops in Chinatown. It was
> never about what you were wearing. It was: Did you bring your
> best game academically with you today and could you contribute
> to the discussion?[17]

For those students who passed the rigorous examination, the competition was only the beginning of what many graduates believed to be an
exceptional educational experience. Yet, in the midst of the achievement and excellence, Hunter also garnered a reputation as a school
where students established close friendships, as well as helping and

inspiring each other. With fewer than 200 students per grade, Hunter was also more intimate than some of the other elite high schools in the city, such as Stuyvesant and Bronx Science.[18]

In a school filled with high-achieving students, Elena Kagan still managed to emerge as one of Hunter College High School's more outstanding students. Kagan is remembered by former students and teachers as someone who appeared destined for great things. Early on, she pursued coursework that centered on legal and constitutional issues, as well as impressing those around her with those qualities and temperament that would be well suited for the law. Stated one classmate in an interview, "She was always very driven. . . . She didn't get sidetracked by feelings."

Kagan also knew how to stand up for herself. One teacher who was known for insulting students in class met his match in Kagan. As a classmate described it years later, "When he would ask a question that I think he half the time assumed was an unanswerable question, she would answer it, and just look at him as if to say, 'Is that all you have?'" Another classmate, in a 2010 interview, offered that "Honestly, if you had asked us back then who among you would be a Supreme Court justice some day, she'd certainly be on the short list. . . . She was always very thoughtful, deliberate and focused and got along with everyone without any drama. Everybody liked her." One classmate, years later, even went so far as to declare that Kagan's aspirations were destined, remarking that Kagan dreamt of becoming a Supreme Court justice. As the classmate stated, "That was a goal from the very beginning. . . . She did talk about it then."[19]

Kagan's need to excel also demonstrated the authority of her mother. In a rare interview years later, Kagan talked about writing and her mother's influence on writing and her studies:

G: What is your very first memory of writing?
K: My first memory of writing is actually having my writing torn apart by my mother.
G: Really?
K: I don't know how old I was, in elementary school or junior high school. But my mother became a teacher. I guess I was in seventh grade when she went back to the classroom. But

before that all her teacher qualities were focused on her kids. And she was a fine writer. She thought it was important that her children be as good writers as they could be. She spent a lot of time going over each sentence in any report that we wrote. That's my first memory of writing: going over each sentence of anything I ever wrote in my early years of school with my mother. . . .

G: Some people consider the kind of severity that you're describing with your mother to turn them off to writing altogether. How did you overcome that?

K: . . . She had very high standards, so if having high standards is some form of severity, then yes, I guess she was severe. But I learned a lot from her and can count many years' worth of students who learned a lot from her. And when I think back about it, I'm glad she did that. I don't know how good a writer I am, but I'm sure I'm much better now than I would've been had she not thought of this as something that was important.[20]

Lessons learned at Hunter were reinforced by daily life realities too. Part of the everyday landscape for Kagan on her way to school was a notorious SRO building located at 75th Street and Broadway known as the Murder Hotel. During the first half of 1974, when Kagan was 14 years old, the building was the scene of a murder, 3 rapes, 14 assaults, 16 robberies, and 16 burglaries. The police called the building the "most crime-ridden building in the city." Its regular tenants consisted of drug dealers, junkies, prostitutes, and their pimps, as well as other petty criminals. It was not uncommon for pedestrians to be hit with garbage from the building's windows; the building's sidewalks stank of urine where people used it as a latrine.

The Kagans resided at the other end of the block from the hotel. When Robert Kagan saw what was happening, he organized his neighbors and began pressing City Hall for some kind of a solution. Still, the neighborhood residents continued to lobby for something to be done; finally, in 1975, the city, using an old electrical code violation, ordered the Murder Hotel vacated.[21]

LEADER AND NONCONFORMIST

At home and at school, Kagan saw how leadership could make a difference in solving problems. While attending Hunter, she become heavily
involved in the school's political organizations, holding the office of
president of the student government or Government Organization;
she was also appointed to serve on a faculty committee. One of her
teachers offered his observations many years later during a newspaper
interview, declaring that "In assemblies and meetings, I used to watch
her work. . . . She'd stand up on stage and present ideas for votes and
she did it very well. She was very self-confident." But Kagan was not
without weaknesses. She smoked cigarettes, one of the few girls in the
school who indulged. However, smoking might have been her only
vice. During a time when disco and dance clubs reigned in the city,
Kagan and her friends spent many Saturday nights sitting on the steps
of the Metropolitan Museum of Art and talked.[22]

Kagan was also growing a political conscience; she later stated that
"Where I grew up—on Manhattan's Upper West Side—nobody ever
admitted to voting for Republicans," and described officeholders as "real
Democrats—not the closet Republicans that one sees so often these
days but men and women committed to liberal principles and motivated by the ideal of an affirmative and compassionate government."[23]

By her senior year, Kagan had been accepted at Princeton. Her
senior picture hinted at what might be ahead: wearing wire-rimmed
aviator glasses and long hair, Kagan posed on the Student Government group's page wearing a judge's robe and holding a gavel in her
hand. Underneath is a quotation from Justice Felix Frankfurter,
who was appointed to the Supreme Court by Franklin D. Roosevelt:
"Government," it reads, "is itself an art, one of the subtlest of arts."[24]

NOTES

1. Reuvan Blau, "Ford To City: Drop Dead: President's Snub Inspired, Not Discouraged, Ex-Gov. Hugh Carey," NY Daily News, August 8, 2011, http://articles.nydailynews.com/2011–08–08/news/298
82248_1_felix-rohatyn-president-ford-unions.

2. "New York City Blackout, 1977," June 27, 2000, http://black out.gmu.edu/events/tl1977.html.

3. John Podhoretz, "The Upper West Side, Then and Now," *Commentary Magazine*, May 2010, http://www.commentarymagazine.com/article/the-upper-west-side-then-and-now/.

4. Ibid.

5. Ibid.

6. Gloria Teal, "The Spark that Lit the Gay Rights Movement, Four Decades Later," Need to Know, June 30, 2010, http://www.pbs.org/wnet/need-to-know/culture/the-spark-that-lit-the-gay-rights-movement-four-decades-later/1873/.

7. Blanche Weisen Cook, "Bella Azbug," 1997, http://www.jewish virtuallibrary.org/jsource/biography/abzug.html.

8. Ibid.

9. Amy Goldstein, Carol D. Leonnig, and Peter Slevin, "For Supreme Court Nominee Elena Kagan, a History of Pragmatism over Partisanship," *Washington Post*, May 11, 2010, http://www.washingtonpost.com/wp-dyn/content/article/2010/05/10/AR2010051002787.html?sid=ST2010080505264; Sheryl Gay Stolberg, Katherien Q. Seelye, and Lisa W. Foderaro, "Pragmatic New Yorker Chose A Careful Path to Washington," *New York Times*, May 11, 2010, Section A, p. 1.

10. Lisa Foderaro, "Growing Up, Kagan Tested Boundaries of Her Faith," *New York Times*, May 12, 2010, http://www.nytimes.com/2010/05/13/nyregion/13synagogue.html?_r=0.

11. Rabbi Arthur O. Waskow, "Bat Mitzvah," n.d., http://www.myjewishlearning.com/life/Life_Events/BarBat_Mitzvah/History/Bat_Mitzvah.shtml.

12. Foderaro, "Growing Up, Kagan Tested Boundaries of Her Faith."

13. Ibid.

14. Ibid.

15. Ibid.

16. Stolberg, Seelye, and Foderaro, "Pragmatic New Yorker Chose A Careful Path to Washington."

17. Katherine Q. Seelye, Lisa W. Foderara, and Sheryl Gay Stolberg, "A Climb Marked by Confidence and Canniness," *New York Times*, May 10, 2010, http://www.nytimes.com/2010/05/10/us/politics/10kagan.html?pagewanted=all&_r=0.

18. Sharon Otterman, "Court Pick Can Still Rise on Her High School Alumni's List," *New York Times*, May 10, 2010, http://www.ny times.com/2010/05/11/nyregion/11hunter.html.

19. Stolberg, Seelye, and Foderaro, "Pragmatic New Yorker Chose A Careful Path to Washington"; Goldstein, Leonnig, and Slevin, "For Supreme Court Nominee Elena Kagan, a History of Pragmatism over Partisanship"; Seelye, Foderara, and Stolberg, "A Climb Marked by Confidence and Canniness."

20. Bryan Garner, "Kagan's Teachers," *ABA Journal* 98, no. 9 (September 2012): 25–26.

21. Michael Daly, "Educated in School and on City's Streets," *New York Daily News*, May 11, 2010, p. 6.

22. Seelye, Foderara, and Stolberg, "A Climb Marked by Confidence and Canniness."

23. Ibid.

24. Ibid.

Chapter 3

COLLEGE YEARS

Gloria Kagan's pushing her daughter paid off; Elena Kagan took to heart her mother's wishes in getting a good education. Looking back, Kagan reflected that her time at Hunter College High School proved to be one of the most formative experiences in her life. As she later recounted in a rare interview, "It was a very cool thing to be a smart girl, as opposed to some other, different kind. . . . And I think that made a great deal of difference to me growing up and in my life afterward." In 1977, Kagan graduated, having been accepted at Princeton University, one of the most prestigious schools in the United States. It was there that Kagan hoped to begin her studies that would eventually lead her to law school. The move also marked a dramatic change of scene, as she prepared to leave behind the energy and chaos of New York City for the small college town of Princeton, New Jersey.[1]

"IN THE NATION'S SERVICE"

Chartered in 1746 as the College of New Jersey, Princeton University was the fourth college established in British North America. It had been chartered in the name of King George II "for the Education of

Youth in the Learned Languages and in the Liberal Arts and Sciences."
Its doors were to be open to all students, "any different sentiments in
religion notwithstanding." The purpose of the college was to train men
who would become "ornaments of the State as well as the Church."[2]

The institution was originally located in Elizabeth, New Jersey,
where its first president, the Reverend Jonathan Dickinson, also served
as pastor of the town's Presbyterian church. Unfortunately, Dickinson
died within a few months after the school opened its doors. In May
1747, Reverend Aaron Burr, then-pastor of the Presbyterian church in
Newark, was persuaded to take on the duties as president of the college.
Burr then decided to move the college to Newark that fall; by spring of
1748, the college had its first graduating class of six young men.[3]

In the fall of 1756, Burr moved the college to Princeton. The students and their teachers were housed in Nassau Hall, then one of the
largest stone buildings built in America. The land for the school was
donated by Nathaniel Fitz Randolph; the building's name was from the
House of Nassau, the family of then English king and prince of Orange,
William III. The building would have other functions besides that of
an educational institution. During the Revolutionary War, Nassau Hall
served as a military hospital or barracks that housed both British and
American troops.[4]

At war's end, Nassau Hall was the scene also of important political
gatherings, including the first session of the New Jersey state legislature
and the Continental Congress. The college received its current name
in 1896, when the school's continued expansion of its courses elevated
the school to university status. The College of New Jersey was officially renamed Princeton University in honor of its host community
of Princeton.[5]

The college was located in the township of Princeton, a small city
numbering approximately 30,000 residents. The town was in a prime
location geographically, being almost equidistant from the large cit-
ies of New York and Philadelphia. In addition to being the home of
Princeton University, the town also was the center for a number of
established and prestigious businesses and corporations, including the
Institute for Advanced Study, Westminster Choir College, Princeton
Theological Seminary, Educational Testing Service which develops
and administers such tests as the SAT, Bristol-Myers Squibb, a global

biopharmaceutical company, Berlitz International which creates and develops language programs and books, and the financial publisher, Dow Jones & Company.

WELCOME, WOMEN!

Throughout much of its history, Princeton had gained a reputation for being an "old boys club," in that the presence of women was highly discouraged; so much so that, as one wag noted, Princeton was said to pretend that women not only did not matter, they simply did not exist. However, this is not entirely true. As early as 1887, with the establishment of Evelyn College, a women's higher learning institution, Princeton hoped to forge the kind of mutual relationship with the school much as Harvard had done with Radcliffe Collage or Columbia University with Barnard College. Unfortunately, the association with Princeton was not enough to help Evelyn College succeed; not more than 10 years after it first opened its doors, Evelyn College closed, due to lack of financial support and help from Princeton.[6]

The drought of female students and professors continued for over 50 years. Finally, in 1942, Elda Emma Anderson arrived at the Princeton Physics Department in the position of a visiting research associate. A year later, in 1943, five more women came to teach in the Language Department as instructors of Turkish and various European and Slavic languages. This was followed by the arrival of Helen Baker, in 1948, to serve as associate director of the Industrial Relations Section. Baker's tenure at the college is also notable because of her appointment as the first woman given the rank above instructor; she was appointed an associate professor by the board of trustees.[7]

Slowly, female students began appearing on campus. Although, the wives and daughters of Princeton faculty members had been allowed to sit in on courses, it would not be until World War II that Princeton, if not welcoming, at least allowed the first female students to enroll. In this case, 23 women were permitted enrollment in a government-sponsored course in photogrammetry, or the study of determining geometric characteristics of objects based on photographs. In 1947, the college allowed three female staff members of the library to enroll in a course to learn the Russian language, so that they could better handle the recently enlarged Russian literature section of the Princeton Library. But the reality of allowing women to graduate from Princeton was more than two decades away.[8]

In 1961, Sabra Follett Meservey was accepted by the Princeton graduate program in Oriental Studies; Meservey became the first woman enrolled in the school's graduate studies program as a full-time degree candidate. However, it was later noted that her letter of acceptance began with the salutation "Dear Sir." Meservey was undeterred and later became the first woman to be granted a master's degree from Princeton. A year after Meservey's acceptance, eight more women enrolled as graduate students at Princeton, and in 1964 Dr. T'sai-ying Cheng, a student in biochemical sciences, became the first woman in the college's history to receive a Doctor of Philosophy degree.[9]

With the introduction of the Critical Languages Program (CLP) in 1963, women were admitted to Princeton as full-time undergraduate students. The CLP provided a program in which students from other colleges could come to Princeton to immerse themselves for a year studying Arabic, Chinese, Japanese, Persian, Russian, and Turkish languages and their related regional studies. Five women were admitted to the CLP, and were soon nicknamed Critters by the male residents. But despite the fact that the women were full-time students, the school still would not allow them to graduate with a Princeton degree, as the CLP program was only of a year's duration.[10]

AN OLD TRADITION FOUNDERS

By the late 1960s, as other all-male Ivy League institutions slowly relented and began admitting women, the Princeton administration began to consider their own options. One was to forge a working relationship with Sarah Lawrence College, an all-women school located in Yonkers, New York; but Princeton, in the end, rejected the proposal. In 1967, the then-president of the college, Robert F. Gohleen, commissioned a committee to study whether admitting women to Princeton as full-time undergraduate degree candidates was possible and feasible. Two years later, in January 1969, the committee issued its report noting that "the presence of talented young women at

Princeton would enhance the total educational experience and contribute to a better balanced social and intellectual life." In addition, the committee also believed that admitting women to the campus would "sustain Princeton's ability to attract outstanding students," something that the school had been struggling with, in part because of its all-male campus and the fact that Princeton compared to other Ivy League schools was seen as stiff, stodgy, and overly conservative. Later that year, the trustees voted 24–8 to formally allow Princeton to admit women as undergraduate students, just in time for the fall semester.[11]

In September 1969, 101 female freshman and 70 female transfer students came to Princeton as members of the student body. In a very short time, they made their presence known and felt. In a 1973 article, the *New York Times* described some of the many achievements women in Princeton's first four-year coeducational class had amassed. For instance, Marsha H. Levy became the first woman to win the Pyne Prize, which was usually given to a senior who has exhibited both academic and extracurricular excellence (not more than three years later, a future Supreme Court justice and Princeton student, Sonya Sotomayor, would receive the award). Levy would also later become one of the college's alumni trustee. That same year saw the school's Marshall scholarship winner awarded to a woman; in addition, of the three of Princeton's Fulbright scholars chosen, one was female.[12]

At the same time that women were entering in increasing numbers as students, so did the number of women tapped to work in the school's administration. In 1971, the school appointed its first two female trustees; a year later, another woman was appointed dean of student affairs, becoming the first female dean in Princeton's history. By the time Elena Kagan was admitted, Princeton had a female dean of the graduate school and a dean of the college, the school's second and third oldest deanships.[13]

There were holdouts to the new standard; most notably, four of the school's elite eating clubs which remained as one of the last bastions of men-only institutions on the campus. It took a lawsuit filed against three of the clubs—the Cottage, Ivy, and Tiger Inn—which refused membership to a female student to finally force the issue. In the spring of 1991, with the state's courts ruling against the segregation of the sexes, even the eating clubs had fallen in line.[14]

PRINCETON DAYS

When Kagan entered Princeton in the fall of 1977, she was 17 years old, which made her younger than most of the freshman on campus. She quickly settled in, declaring a major in history, with an emphasis on political history, especially the history of labor movements and radical politics. She soon earned a reputation as a committed student with a sincere passion for politics. Kagan, a committed Democrat, also found time to become involved in politics, serving as a legislative intern for Representative Ted Weiss. She was also known to favor vodka tonics and, on a few occasions, was known to have gotten drunk. Many classmates found her to be a curious combination of both "vivacious and reserved."

However, one classmate, Christopher Chambers had a very different impression of Kagan as he noted years later:

> When I was a junior at Princeton I took two history classes with Kagan (she was a graduating senior in my department). From contact and observation, I concluded, maybe pigheadedly, four things about her. First, that she was a brilliant student. Second, she was very funny. Third, she seemed more comfortable with the minutia of political and social justice, rather than the broader cultural and power themes. And fourth, she was a walking stereotype of an Upper West Side Manhattan liberal. Here's the rub: the line between such liberals and "Neo-cons" is razor thin.[15]

Perhaps the one professor at Princeton who had an opportunity to get to know Kagan personally and professionally was Sean Wilentz, who was early in his career as a historian when he first met Kagan in one of his classes. Even then, Wilentz recalled, Kagan stood out among his students describing her as "at once brilliant and skeptical of dogma, with an unusually mature way of thinking that would not settle for easy answers to historical problems." Wilentz also stated that Kagan was "witty, engaging [and] down-to-earth."[16]

Kagan herself credits Wilentz with helping her not only to become a better thinker, but also in challenging her to be a better writer. In a rare interview, Kagan recalled Wilentz as a "very fine historian" who:

> spent so much time not just trying to teach me how to be a good historian but really trying to teach me to be a good writer. He would mark up my thesis during my senior year at Princeton. . . . That experience was probably the first time in my life when somebody who himself was a fabulous writer spent so much time, sentence by sentence, telling me what I could do better.[17]

Kagan was also known as an extremely organized and thorough student with an eye for detail, as seen in her almost habitual note-taking which would soon come in handy when she went to work on the school newspaper the *Daily Princetonian*. Still, in spite of her wit and humor, Kagan was also guarded, particularly when it came to discussing her political views and her social life. Her friends tended to be other students with strong intellectual leanings, many of whom gravitated toward working on the school newspaper or being active in student government. Yet, even as her friends were protesting for the school to divest itself of its holding in an apartheid South Africa, Kagan remained more detached. Still, even with those off-limits areas of her life and her refusal to be drawn into personal or political discussions, Wilentz noted that Kagan was someone "you'd like to have . . . as a friend."[18]

THE DAILY PRINCETONIAN

During her junior year, Kagan had undertaken a grueling schedule. After attending morning classes, she then retreated to a small office in the newsroom of the campus newspaper, the *Daily Princetonian*; Kagan had begun working on the newspaper as a reporter as a freshman. Then, in her junior year, she ran for the top spot as editor; she lost but as runner-up was chosen to head up the editorial writing team. The paper prided itself on its independent status; as editorial chairwoman, one of Kagan's duties was to help write the opinion content and unsigned editorials on a wide variety of topics. She was known in the newsroom for her writing at blinding speed opinions and editorial pieces on the university and its policies. Kagan's quick take on matters and skillful writing rapidly established her as a valued member of the newsroom staff. As a classmate remembered, "We didn't have PCs available to edit as we were drafting. . . . But she [Elena] could just sit down at a little manual Royal typewriter and punch out incredibly well-written advocacy pieces in a short amount of time."[19]

For Steven Bernstein, the chairman of the paper, appointing Kagan as editorial chairperson was not a difficult decision. Bernstein had long been impressed by Kagan's writing and her intellectual capabilities. In a 2010 interview, Bernstein stated that "Elena was an obvious choice for me as editorial page editor because she formulated her opinions beautifully, even back then. . . . They were very tightly reasoned, clearly thought-out, fair, forceful, cogent." But, even though Kagan spent most of her evenings working at the paper, Bernstein also pointed out that she did not write all the editorials herself but instead chose to work with others. "That wasn't her style . . . She was a very collaborative person," Bernstein emphasized later. In fact, consensus was not only desired in the writing of the paper's editorials, it was policy; not unlike the judicial bench she would later ascend to, at the *Daily Princetonian*, editorials at the paper were not sent for publication until a majority consensus was reached. Kagan's editorials were also earmarked by the fact that they often read like legal briefs.

"She strongly considered viewpoints," said Marc Fisher, a *Washington Post* columnist who was a classmate of Kagan's at Princeton. "There were no rants . . . She [was] not a partisan animal." Steven Bernstein, who worked with her, remembered that Kagan always approached positions and potential controversy with calm reasoning: "She might argue something quite passionately, but it was thoughtful and reasoned. . . . [Her opinions were] informed by evidence and data and not just feelings . . . "[20]

THE MAKING OF A JUSTICE

Many years later, looking at the 70 or so newspaper clips written by Kagan allows the reader an invaluable look at Kagan's thinking and ideas. As one reporter later noted, the inventory demonstrates "how clearly her passions and beliefs show through. What emerges is a portrait of an earnest liberal, concerned especially with issues of gender, equality, and identity politics. [In addition,] all the greatest hits of late '70s, early '80s boomer liberalism are here."[21]

Those topics ran the gamut from reporting about a group of students defending themselves against marijuana charges; to union grievances; as well as the ongoing efforts to diversify Princeton's eating clubs. The editorials also called for the school to withdraw investments in South Africa because of its apartheid policies, as well as asking for better protection for workers at nuclear facilities. More than a dozen of the editorial and op-ed pieces focused on women's rights, including a piece about how one eating club drenched an activist with beer to another editorial which presented a pleasing profile of Princeton's unofficial "dean of women." In 1980, Kagan called for the creation of a women's studies department on the campus, writing: "Traditional academia has, for the most part, failed to establish a base of knowledge about women and their roles. . . . Women's studies can fill this gap and, at the same time, serve as a truly valuable intellectual approach to a great variety of older disciplines, whether history, politics, literature or art."[22]

In another instance, the newspaper took the university to task when the school became involved in a lawsuit in early 1980 over whether it had the right to control whether or not nonaffiliated organizations or speakers could come to the campus. The paper's editorial described the school administration's policy "frightening," stating that the idea of academic freedom is "the freedom of academia to take unpopular and provocative stands rather than . . . the freedom of the entire university to remain immune from any type of government interference."[23]

Some of the pieces do reveal Kagan's personal views. In one personal essay, written after the 1980 elections which elected Republican Ronald Reagan to the presidency, entitled "Fear and Loathing in Brooklyn," Kagan described herself as having "absorbed . . . liberal principles early . . . [and] I have retained them fairly intact to this day." In writing about the victory of conservative Republicans elected to Congress in that same election, Kagan noted:

Even after the returns came in, I found it hard to conceive of the victories of these anonymous but Moral Majority-backed opponents of Senators Church, McGovern, Bayh and Culver, these

avengers of "innocent life" and the B-1 bomber, these beneficiaries of a general turn to the right and a profound disorganization
on the left. . . . In my more rational moments, I can now argue
that the next few years will be marked by American disillusion-
ment with conservative programs and solutions, and that a new,
revitalized, perhaps more leftist left will once again come to the
fore.[24]

Kagan also wrote several sports stories during her time at the newspaper, covering football, hockey, basketball, tennis, and baseball. However, the tone of the pieces is such that she often taunts the teams
more for their losses than their victories. Still, Kagan was not without
humor as seen in her senior year when she notes in a "farewell from
the editors" piece that "noble ideals die quickly in a newsroom," and
"The camaraderie of a newsroom? You mention that on law school ap-
plications." She also confessed as to why she really wrote the editorial
pieces:

So, why bother? Well, as reluctant as we are to admit it, we've
taken a certain pride in putting out this page over the past year.
And we'd like to think that at least a few of you out there were
reading. There's just one more reason: it's given us a ready excuse
not to start our theses.[25]

TAKING A STAND

Despite the very liberal tone of the editorials in the *Daily Princetonian*, Kagan continued to be politically restrained in her dealings
with her classmates and fellow reporters and editors. Steven Bernstein stated later in an interview that in spite of the long hours the
two worked together and the many discussions over current events
and politics they had, he could never recall one incident in which
Kagan expressed her political views. Bernstein even said he was un-
sure as to whether or not Kagan was even a registered voter. There
was also the fact that as a member of the newspaper staff, Kagan was
prohibited from participation in any political displays. As Bernstein
stated, "I don't remember her participating in marching, protesting,

things like that. . . . I would probably describe her back then—her politics—as progressive and thoughtful but well within the mainstream of the . . . sort of liberal, democratic, progressive tradition, and everything with lower case."[26]

Sean Wilentz, Kagan's mentor agreed, noting that even though he did discuss politics and events with Kagan, he was never able to get a strong sense of her political radar because of her abilities as a journalist, which added to her general reserve and discretion in discussing personal politics. Still, Kagan may have been discreet about her own views, but that did not mean she was alienated from the thriving atmosphere of political activism on campus. In April 1980, her senior year, Kagan, Elliot Spitzer (who would one day become governor of New York), and six other campus leaders—all members of the Coordinating Council of the Campaign for a Democratic University—created and signed a manifesto that appeared in the *Daily Princetonian*. In the document, the group pushed for a "fundamental restructuring of University governance," stating that they believed that the administration at Princeton rules this campus by decree. Decisions affecting all aspects of undergraduate student life are made unilaterally by Nassau Hall (the central administration building), and that "effective student participation in University governance is a myth."

The manifesto went on to cite a case where students were able to build opposition to a proposed ban on pornography on campus when they accidently learned of the plan. As the piece further pointed out: "This case typifies how the administration makes decisions." Further, the student leaders pointed out that "Discussions are held behind closed doors; students are 'consulted' only after Nassau Hall has reached its decision and agreed to a uniform position."[27]

If Kagan remained fairly circumspect about her political activities on the Princeton campus, she was more engaged when away from the school. In addition to her internship with Ted Weiss, Kagan also served as a deputy press secretary for the campaign of Elizabeth Holtzman, a New York Congresswoman who was running for the Senate, during the summer of 1980. The work was intense, with Kagan often working 14-hour days in her duties. When Holtzman lost in the November election, Kagan was bitter. Writing a week later for an op-ed piece for the paper, she stated, "Self-pity still sneaks up. . . . And I wonder how all this could possibly have happened and where on earth I'll be able to get a job next year."[28]

"TO THE FINAL CONFLICT"

As part of her requirements for graduation in her senior year, Kagan was to write a senior thesis on a historical topic. Working with Sean Wilentz, Kagan decided to study the Socialist Party in New York City. She conducted her research by diligently combing through library archives to piece together the story. Her finished product was a 156-page thesis, titled "To the Final Conflict: Socialism in New York City, 1900–1933." In telling the story of the Socialist party in America, Kagan noted that "Americans are more likely to speak of a golden past than of a golden future, of capitalism's glories than of socialism's greatness. . . . Conformity overrides dissent; the desire to conserve has overwhelmed the urge to alter. Such a state of affairs cries out for explanation." Further, in analyzing the history of the Socialist Party in the United States, Kagan saw the movement's end as a "sad but also a chastening one for those who, more than half a century after socialism's decline, still wish to change America . . . In unity lies their only hope." Among the many points that Kagan argues is that the lack of a strong socialist movement in the United States was due in part to mistakes made by the party as opposed to other external factors which many before believed led to the party's demise.[29]

Wilentz later asserted the Kagan's work demonstrated the "futility of dogma" and how it led to the collapse of the Socialist movement in the United States. Many years later, when Kagan's thesis was resurrected and the subject of intense scrutiny by conservatives, Wilentz stated simply that "Sympathy for the movement of people who were trying to better their lives isn't something to look down on. . . . Studying something doesn't necessarily mean that you endorse it. It means you're into it. That's what historians do." Many years later, another political writer agreed, writing that "The thesis is a piece of history, quite good, and quite confident in dismissing the opinions of scholars of the movement like Daniel Bell (a noted sociologist and socialist)." The writer also noted that Kagan does write from a somewhat sympathetic position, but more important, the document shows Kagan as carefully considering the facts and providing a practical and common sense conclusion about the story of the Socialist Party.[30]

However, the thesis may have been more personal than people realized for Kagan. In her acknowledgement, she offers thanks to her brother Marc, whose "involvement in radical causes led me to explore the history of American radicalism in the hope of clarifying my own political ideas." For Kagan, the thesis may have simply been, in part, an extension of conversations between her father and her brother, who both were sympathetic to the Socialist Party. In addition, Marc Kagan would eventually eschew his Upper West Side upbringing to go to work as an employee of the New York City Transit Authority as well as becoming an active union reformer in Transport Workers Local 100.[31]

MOVING ON

In the spring of 1981, Elena Kagan graduated from Princeton *summa cum laude*, or with highest honors. In addition, Kagan was also awarded the Daniel M. Sachs Class of 1960 Graduating Scholarship. The award allowed the student the opportunity to study at the prestigious Worcester College at the University of Oxford, England, for two years. The award would pay a stipend and tuition. Although Kagan still was focused on law school, this opportunity was too great to pass up. Law school, for now, could wait another two years. By the fall of 1981, Kagan was back in college, this time in England.

NOTES

1. "Elena Kagan. Biography," Bio. True Story, 2013, http://www.biography.com/people/elena-kagan-560228.

2. Princeton University, "Princeton University at a Glance," n.d., http://www.princeton.edu/main/about/history/glance/.

3. Ibid.

4. Ibid.

5. Ibid.

6. "The History of Women at Princeton University," Princeton University Library, January 18, 2013, http://libguides.princeton.edu/content.php?pid=15189&sid=625907.

7. Ibid.

8. Ibid.

9. Ibid.

10. Ibid.

11. Ibid.

12. Ibid.

13. Ibid.

14. Ibid.

15. "Elena Kagan's College Years: At Princeton She Was Both 'Vivacious' and Reserved," *Huffington Post*, May 5, 2010, http://www.huffingtonpost.com/2010/05/05/elena-kagans-college-year_n_564894.html; Christopher Chambers, "Elena Kagan Is No Thurgood Marshall," *Grio*, May 11, 2010, http://thegrio.com/2010/05/11/why-elena-kagan-is-no-thurgood-marshall/.

16. Cass Cliatt, "Princeton Alumna Kagan Nominated to Supreme Court," *News at Princeton*, May 10, 2010, http://www.princeton.edu/main/news/archive/S27/34/66S12/index.xml?section=topstories.

17. Bryan A. Garner, "Kagan's Teachers: 9th Justice Talks about Her Influences in Writing, Reading and Reasoning," *Aba Journal*, September 1, 2012, http://www.abajournal.com/magazine/article/kagans_teachers_9th_justice_talks_about_her_influences_in_writing_reading/.

18. Amy Goldstein, Carol D. Leonnig, and Peter Slevin, "For Supreme Court Nominee Elena Kagan, a History of Pragmatism over Partisanship," *Washington Post*, May 11, 2010, http://www.washingtonpost.com/wp-dyn/content/article/2010/05/10/AR2010051002787.html?sid=ST2010080505264; Ameena Schelling, "Reserved Passion: Kagan '81," *Daily Princetonian*, May 3, 2010, 2011, http://www.dailyprincetonian.com/2010/05/03/26081/.

19. Goldstein, Leonnig, and Slevin, "For Supreme Court Nominee Elena Kagan, a History of Pragmatism over Partisanship"; Rohan Mascarenhas, "U.S. Supreme Court Nominee Elena Kagan's Writings, Views while at Princeton to Be Examined Published: Monday," *Star-Ledger*, May 10, 2010, http://www.nj.com/news/index.ssf/2010/05/us_supreme_court_nominee_elena.

20. Schelling, "Reserved Passion"; Mascarenhas, "U.S. Supreme Court Nominee Elena Kagan's Writings."

21. "Elena Kagan: Cub Reporter," *Daily Beast*, May 19, 2010, http://www.thedailybeast.com/newsweek/2010/05/19/elena-kagan-cub-reporter.html.

22. Mascarenhas, "U.S. Supreme Court Nominee Elena Kagan's Writings."

23. Schelling, "Reserved Passion."

24. Mascarenhas, "U.S. Supreme Court Nominee Elena Kagan's Writings."

25. "Elena Kagan: Cub Reporter."

26. Schelling, "Reserved Passion."

27. Ibid.

28. Mascarenhas, "U.S. Supreme Court Nominee Elena Kagan's Writings."

29. Schelling, "Reserved Passion."

30. Ibid.; Heather Horn, "Elena Kagan's Senior Thesis: 'Socialism' and Beyond," *Atlantic Wire*, May 17, 2010, http://www.theatlantic wire.com/politics/2010/05/elena-kagan-s-senior-thesis-socialism-and-beyond/24435/.

31. Schelling, "Reserved Passion."

Chapter 4

LEARNING THE LAW

Worcester College is one of 38 colleges affiliated with Oxford University, located in Oxford, England, in the central southern region of England. Oxford University has the distinction of being the second oldest university in the world and is the oldest educational institution in Great Britain. For the next two years, Elena Kagan would come to call the city and the college home as she continued her studies.

Worcester has an old and distinguished pedigree as well. The school had been an institution of learning since the 13th century, when as Gloucester House, established in 1283 by the Benedictine Abbey of St. Peter at Gloucester, served to educate 13 monks of the Benedictine order. In time, other Benedictine Houses wished to provide the same educational opportunities to their monks, and so petitioned the Abbey at Gloucester to share the building. In the process, to accommodate the growing number of students, more buildings were constructed. By 1539, when the monasteries were dissolved and Gloucester College ceased to exist, 15 abbeys of the Benedictine order were educating their monks at Gloucester.[1]

Three years later, in 1542, the former Gloucester College buildings were granted to the first bishop of Oxford, Robert King, who used the buildings and grounds as a personal residence until moving to the palace at St. Aldate. In 1560, the buildings were then sold to Sir Thomas White, the founder of St John's College; the college and grounds became known as Gloucester Hall. Unfortunately, the college's fortunes never improved and in fact steadily declined. Then, in 1714, Gloucester Hall was reestablished as Worcester College, named after a local nobleman, Sir Thomas Cookes, who left a sum of money for the establishment of a new college. By 1720, new construction was underway at the college, but because funding was spotty, the construction of new buildings took longer than expected. Somehow, the buildings and grounds were completed, and today the school boasts one of the finest landscapes with beautiful gardens and a distinctive array of buildings that span the college's and the country's architectural history.[2]

THE DEVELOPMENT AND EROSION OF THE AMERICAN EXCLUSIONARY RULE

While at Oxford, Kagan settled into her classes. She tended to spend her time with students who were more interested in political theory, rather than students studying pre-law; this interest would carry over into her later studies at law school. She also found time to become the coxswain for a women's crew team: the position meant that Kagan was in charge of the boat, especially with the navigation and steering. Kagan relished her role in leading the eight rowers on the team; as one Princeton friend later described it, Kagan "was leading people who had physical talents beyond hers—the idea of a leadership role where you are part of a team."[3]

As part of her graduation requirement, Kagan was also required to write a thesis, similar to her efforts at Princeton under her history professor Sean Wilentz. To meet this requirement, Kagan undertook the study and writing of a 125-page thesis paper called "The Development and Erosion of the American Exclusionary Rule: A Study in Judicial Method." The thesis presented an analytical and critical look at the idea of the exclusionary rule and its evolution on the U.S. Supreme Court, and in particular the Warren Court during the period 1953–1969.

Kagan tackled one of the most important and valued legal precepts in American law. The exclusionary rule states that under constitutional law any evidence collected or analyzed in violation of a defendant's constitutional rights can be inadmissible for criminal prosecution in a court of law. The principle is rooted firmly in the Fourth Amendment and was created to protect citizens from illegal search or seizure by law enforcement authorities. The rule also draws on the Fifth Amendment, which protects a person from incriminating themselves as well as the Sixth Amendment which guarantees the right of a person to legal counsel.

THE WARREN COURT

Given Kagan's background and own political sensibilities, her interest in the Warren Court seemed a suitable choice. From 1953 until 1969, Earl Warren, appointed to the Supreme Court under President Dwight Eisenhower, crafted a court bench that actively used the principle of judicial review to scrutinize and, in many instances, overturn state and federal statutes on a wide variety of cases. During his tenure as chief justice, Warren oversaw such landmark cases, such as 1954's *Brown v. Board of Education*, which struck down school segregation and gave momentum to the modern Civil Rights Movement and the Civil Rights Act of 1964. In the case of *Reynolds v. Sims*, decided in 1964, the court ruled that state legislatures were to be apportioned on the basis of population rather than geographic areas, which saw a major shift in political power moving from sparsely populated rural areas to the more densely populated urban areas. The court also struck down the century-old practices of poll taxes, unfair residency requirements, and property qualifications as well as allowing for third party candidates to be featured on ballots.[4]

But it was in the area of criminal procedure that the Warren Court was probably at its most controversial. In the 1963 decision, *Gideon v. Wainwright*, the court ruled that criminal defendants were to be provided with attorneys in the event they could not afford one. The court also stated that defendants who were impoverished should not be denied the right to appeal their cases. Perhaps, one of the most important court cases with regard to the rights of a criminally accused defendant came with the landmark 1966 court decision *Miranda v. Arizona*. The decision laid the groundwork for the creation of the *Miranda* warning in which police must inform any person under arrest of their constitutional rights, which includes the right to counsel, and the right to not self-incriminate by answering questions. These decisions, along with others, radically changed the makeup of the American criminal justice system, leading many critics of the court to charge that criminals had more rights than their victims.[5]

The court went on to state opinions on a wide variety of other legal issues, including compulsory loyalty oaths (the court found them vague and unsuitable), free speech protection under the First Amendment (especially given the growing antiwar sympathies of many Americans against the Vietnam War), and supporting the right to demonstrate at state capitols, in the streets, and at segregated facilities in the South. The court challenged state laws regarding slander and libel, which often were smoke screens to discourage open debate on controversial issues, and ruled that persons who hold public office or are public figures, such as celebrities, must prove that defamation or false statements were made with actual malice or the knowledge that the information about the person was knowingly false. In religious cases, the Warren Court struck down the recitation of state-written prayers in public schools, as well as the idea that a person seeking public office had to publicly declare a belief in God as a prerequisite to hold office and that an individual did not need to believe in God in order to obtain a Conscientious Objector status.[6]

Next to the *Miranda* decision, the Supreme Court's ruling in the case of *Griswold v. Connecticut* in 1965 was one of the most significant decisions the court wrote. In their ruling, the court struck down a Connecticut state law which prohibited the distribution of birth control information, stating that individuals had a right to privacy. The decision is also notable in that it laid the groundwork for the landmark court ruling in 1973 of *Roe v. Wade* which gave women the right to have abortions.[7]

The Warren Court set the U.S. Supreme Court on a path that demonstrated a strong commitment to change; rather than responding to pressures by other branches of the government or political groups, the Warren Court instead became a court of reform, and an active one at that. The court clearly demonstrated its liberal affinity to protecting the civil rights of many groups, including African Americans and women, as well as showing a keen interest in the protection of criminal offenders. Warren was well aware that he had raised the ire of many conservative political groups, as well as the more conservative branch of the judiciary who charged that the Warren Court had clearly overstepped its boundaries in interpretation of the Constitution and Bill of Rights. But, as the Warren court demonstrated in decision after decision, its aim was to promote a more equal society.[8]

KAGAN'S ARGUMENT

In her thesis, Kagan examined the exclusionary rule and how it was interpreted by the Supreme Court, beginning in 1913, when the exclusionary rule was first enacted and how, by the time of the Warren Court, the exclusionary rule was being used not only by federal courts, but also mandated by state courts. Kagan also showed how the Supreme Court interpreted the theory of the exclusionary rule no less than four different ways, two of which were based on constitutional law, the other two not. The end result was what Kagan described as "doctrinal confusion."[9]

Kagan went on to state that the orthodox or conventional view of the judicial branch of the government, as outlined by Alexander Hamilton in the *Federalist Papers*, was that of a passive government body, conceived to maintain and uphold the laws of the land rather than acting as a legislative body and enacting new laws. To Kagan, utilizing the court in this way was "largely negative and a restraining role" that hindered the court from doing more.[10]

A good portion of the thesis is focused on the Warren Court, a court that Kagan described as "a court with a mission . . . to correct the social injustices and inequalities of American life . . . [and] to transform the nation." Further, Kagan stated that "the Warren Court justices set themselves a goal . . . and they steered by this goal when resolving individual cases," especially as it pertained to the rectifying of social injustices. Kagan also praised the Warren Court's ethical sense, in that the court as a living institution was dealing with living problems. As such, the court could not be expected to achieve perfect logical symmetry, for "logic overdone can stultify all its touches." Further, the court refused to confine itself to the earlier held ideas of what a judiciary branch should do. By "refus[ing] to confine itself, [the Warren Court] felt a positive duty to assume an active role in the government process," and that the court did not believe in just "adhering to federalist principles" but rather be actively engaged in the creation of a "just society."[11]

Kagan did not find fault with the Warren Court's vision of a "just and fair society [that] inform[ed] almost the whole of the Court's constitutional analysis." If anything, the Warren Court's decisions closely followed Kagan's own political leanings. Kagan did criticize the court, however, for failing to produce "a tenable legal argument" for its decisions with regard to the exclusionary rule. By not doing that, Kagan suggested the Warren Court left itself vulnerable to reversals or modifications of the decisions by future courts. Finally, Kagan stated: "U.S. Supreme Court justices live in the knowledge that they have the authority to command or to block great social, political and economic change. At times, the temptation to wield this power becomes irresistible. The justices, at such times, will attempt to steer the law in order to achieve certain ends and advance certain values."[12]

Finally, in one of the more controversial statements that Kagan made in her thesis, is what she believed constituted the duty of the justices:

> Judges are judges, but they are also men. . . . As men and as participants in American life, judges will have opinions, prejudices, values. Perhaps most important, judges will have goals. And because this is so, judges will often try to mold and steer the law in order to promote certain ethical values and achieve certain social ends. Such activity is not necessarily wrong or invalid. The law, after all, is a human instrument—an instrument designed to meet men's needs. . . . Concern for ethical values thus has an important role to play in the judicial process. For in the last analysis, the law is a very human enterprise with very human goals.[13]

Kagan's thesis was approved, and in late spring 1983, she graduated from Worcester College with an MPhil in Philosophy. Kagan also learned that she had been accepted into the Harvard Law School program. Years later, as her confirmation hearings were getting underway, Kagan's thesis done at Worcester along with her senior Princeton thesis would provide ample fodder for her opponents and critics, who took Kagan to task for her views about the role of the judiciary as makers of new law rather than as upholders of the law. As Kagan quipped in an interview at that time, "Let me just say that it's dangerous to write a paper about the law before you've spent a day in law school."[14]

HARVARD

Upon returning home, Kagan busily prepared leaving for yet another school, this time in Cambridge, Massachusetts. Her acceptance into Harvard Law School, while an immense accomplishment, was also a bittersweet moment for Kagan's father. Although proud that his daughter was choosing to follow in his footsteps, he was also disappointed that she decided not to go to his alma mater, Yale Law School. By September, Kagan was settling into her new quarters at Harvard.

Established in 1817, Harvard Law School is the oldest continuously operating law school in the United States. The school's early origins began with Isaac Royall, who in 1781 left a large parcel of land to the school with the specific instructions to use the monies gotten from the sale of the land to endow a Professor of Laws at the college. The Royall Chair continues to support a Harvard Law School professor today. In 1806, Royall's heirs sold off the rest of the estate and used the monies to create a school of law at Harvard.[15]

By 1827, the school was struggling with only one student and one professor. Thanks to the help of some former alumnus, the school established the Dane Professorship of Law. The position was given to Joseph Story who, at that time, was the nation's youngest Supreme Court justice (much as Kagan would be over two centuries later). It would be Story who helped define the law school's mission, which included a strong commitment to public service. During the 1870s, the school received help from another important figure: Christopher Columbus Langdell who arrived at the school as the first dean of the Law School. Langdell believed that the study of law should be an interactive one as well as being extremely disciplined; he envisioned the study of law as one which incorporated the Socratic method whereby students were directly challenged by their professors; doing so, Langdell held, would allow the students to analyze cases more sharply and deeply. In order to carry out this vision, new classrooms were needed, and so began an ambitious program of construction on the campus.[16]

The Harvard Law Library also boasts of an impressive history, dating back to 1817, when the School of Law was first formed. By 1820, the law library had a collection of 584 titles; by 1823, the collection expanded when 1,000 books belonging to Joseph Story was added; by 1841, the school had 6,100 volumes, which was enough to allow students "to verify every citation which is made in *Blackstone's Commentaries*," then the standard reference tool for judges and lawyers in the 19th century. By 1960, the library's collection numbered over one million volumes; today, the Harvard Law Library is considered to be one of the best law libraries in the nation.[17]

FIRST YEAR

Elena Kagan was 23 years old when she entered Harvard Law School in the fall of 1983. Armed with a set of impressive credentials, including her *summa cum laude* degree from Harvard and her master's degree from Worcester, Kagan seemed poised to jump in. But her adjustment to the intensely competitive atmosphere of Harvard found Kagan struggling—so much so that by the end of the first semester, Kagan received the two worst grades of her entire law school career—a B in criminal law and a B-minus in her torts class. The grades were at best mediocre, but for an overachiever like Kagan, they may as well have been Fs. According to one friend who was in Kagan's study group, the torts grade was a shock. According to the friend, Kagan had a bad day when taking the exam. In a later interview, he stated, "She was definitely upset about this torts grade—there was no doubt about it. . . . I remember saying to her that in the larger scheme of things it will not loom very large."[18]

Kagan, determined not to let her grades suffer anymore, rebounded admirably by the 1984 spring semester when her grades dramatically improved; she earned three As and three A-minuses. It was a sign of things to come; Kagan would go on to earn 17 As out of the 21 courses she took at Harvard. In two other courses, including an administrative law course in which Kagan would later focus on more intensely as a law scholar, she earned a B-plus. As one of Kagan's professors later wrote, "There's just no doubt that her first-year spring term grades (including those in the 'year' courses), not the fall term ones, are the true reflection of her capacity and her learning. . . . Whatever was in her way on those fall term exams, it wasn't affecting her class performance even during the fall, and evidently was gone by exam time in May." Another professor who had Kagan in his federal courts class was more succinct in his judgment of her abilities: "Her questions were so penetrating that my knees would wobble."[19]

Her summers between school semesters found Kagan continuing to be immersed in the law, as well. During the summer of 1984, Kagan worked as a summer associate in the law offices of Fried, Frank, Harris, Shriver and Jacobson, a Park Avenue firm in New York, where she worked in the litigation department, writing briefs and memoranda. The following summer, Kagan again found a summer associate position, this time with the firm of Paul, Weiss, Rifkind, Wharton and Garrison, where she once more found herself working in litigation and writing legal briefs and memoranda.[20]

Elena Kagan greeting members of the National Association of Women Judges in Cambridge, Massachusetts, on March 9, 2012. (AP Photo/Josh Reynolds)

In her last year in law school, Kagan became supervising editor of the *Harvard Law Review*. During her tenure, Kagan published one of the more controversial articles written by the Harvard law professor, Derrick Bell, an African American legal scholar credited with establishing Critical Race Theory. Bell, who became the first African American tenured professor of law at Harvard, submitted an article entitled "The Civil Rights Chronicles." The essay is a curious mix of fiction and legal theory which argued that the Constitution was—and still remains—tainted by white supremacy. Further, Bell would argue that the nation was awaiting "a common crisis that will overcome racism" that could only be achieved through a radical overhaul of the U.S. Constitution.

The article opens with the following introduction:

> A committee planning the bicentennial anniversary of the Constitution finished a long session reviewing the lives of the men who wrote and signed this nation's basic legal document. Later, the committee's lone minority group member told a wise friend of a recurring fantasy in which he is transported back through time to give the framers a preview of the two centuries of developments in American constitutional law. "If that were to happen," he wondered, "where should I begin so major a teaching task?"
>
> The friend's response was kind. "First," she said gently, "you would have to explain to the framers how you, a black, had gotten free of your chains and gained the audacity to teach white men anything."

From there, Bell, speaking through his fictional alter ego, Geneva Crenshaw, argues how American civil rights law is not aimed at improving the civil rights of African Americans, and when it does happen, it does so only when it serves white self-interest.[21]

In a section of the article entitled "The Chronicle of the Slave Scrolls," Geneva Crenshaw recounts a fable about discovering parchment scrolls on the west coast of Africa inside a model of a slave ship. According to Crenshaw, the scrolls taught the "readily available but seldom read history of slavery in America" by those who had lived through it. The discovery of these scrolls encouraged African Americans to meet in healing groups that motivated them to compete more

fiercely for achievement and respect, that is, until a television minister warns them that the scrolls were inciting racial hatred by teaching
about old evils. Then, came the passage of Racial Toleration Laws by
many states that prohibited any teaching about the history of racial
conflict. In the end, African Americans did nothing.[22]

According to Bell, the solution to the problem of racial injustice
lay in "a substantive due process right that barred government interference with the racial healing sessions," based on the same right to
privacy recognized in *Roe v. Wade*. Further, the right to "racial healing"
would grant special protection to the idea that "the racism of whites
rather than the deficiencies of blacks causes our lowly position in this
society."[23]

Kagan agreed to publish the article, but she cautioned about Bell's
solution. In a handwritten memo, Kagan noted:

> We're a little bit concerned at the focus on this part of the piece.
> The doctrinal section centers on the idea of creating a substan-
> tive due process right to racial healing. But the reader is left won-
> dering: why wouldn't the Court strike these laws down on first
> amendment grounds? It strikes me that the Court would indeed
> strike these laws down on the ground of free speech or free as-
> sociation.[24]

Years later, the query would be held up by Kagan's opponents as evidence of her liberal leanings and acceptance of Bell's Critical Race
Theories, when in fact it would suggest that Kagan was continuing to
analyze and question various aspects of constitutional law.

In the spring of 1986, Elena Kagan graduated from Harvard Law
School; her first semester woes far behind her as she graduated *magna
cum laude*. For the next year, Kagan would spend her time clerking for
Judge Abner Mikva, sitting on the U.S. Court of Appeals, the District
of Columbia circuit.

CLERKING WITH MIKVA

Kagan's opportunity to clerk for Mikva seemed most judicious. Like
Kagan, Mikva came from a liberal background; as a lawyer, he was a

supporter of women's right to choose and gun control while opposing the death penalty. Although many opposed his nomination to the federal appeals court, Mikva, once seated, showed more pragmatism than personal politics on the bench. Among the opinions he rendered, Mikva was known for favoring freedom of speech and consumer rights. He also disagreed with the Supreme Court landmark decision on women's rights to choose, *Roe v. Wade*, stating that he believed that state legislatures were addressing the issue and slowly making progress. While considered outspoken on his views, his more conservative colleagues on the bench found Mikva a willing colleague, open to debate and reason.[25]

Kagan stood out among the close-knit group of clerks in an atmosphere where working late nights was a norm. To take breaks from the intense legal work, Kagan played poker, where she gained a reputation as an excellent player. Despite her small stature (Kagan is barely 5'3" tall) she enjoyed playing basketball with the other clerks. She was also part of the crowd that made regular stops to City Lights in Dupont Circle for Chinese food and as well as guilty runs to a downtown Popeyes for fried chicken.[26]

Although later critics of Kagan would accuse Mikva heavily influenced Kagan, further deepening her liberal stance, others who worked with both stated that it was not the case. One person noted that Kagan was "probably, in her heart of hearts, moderately liberal," but described her approach to the law as "very hard-nosed [and] non-ideologically driven." Kagan would emerge as Mikva's favorite; he called Kagan the "pick of the litter" the year she clerked for him. However, as a friend stated, " there was no sense of sycophancy to her." Many years later, Mikva recalled Kagan as "a good clerk, one of the best. She told me what the law was." He added, "She often ended up on the liberal side. . . . But she had a lot of conservative views. She was big on family values . . . (and) very sensitive to her immigrant traditions."[27]

NOTES

1. "History of the College," Worcester College, n.d., http://www.worc.ox.ac.uk/About-Worcester/History-of-the-College.
2. Ibid.

3. Amy Goldstein, Carol D. Leonnig, and Peter Slevin, "For Supreme Court Nominee Elena Kagan, a History of Pragmatism over Partisanship," *Washington Post*, May 11, 2010, http://www.washingtonpost.com/wp-dyn/content/article/2010/05/10/AR2010051002787.html?sid=ST2010080505264.

4. "The Warren Court," the Supreme Court Historical Society, n.d., http://www.supremecourthistory.org/history-of-the-court/history-of-the-court-2/the-warren-court-1953–1969/.

5. Ibid.

6. Ibid.

7. Ibid.

8. Ibid.

9. Elena Kagan, "The Development and Erosion of the American Exclusionary Rule: A Study in Judicial Method," Oxford University, June 1983, p. 4, http://online.wsj.com/public/resources/documents/kagan1983thesis.pdf.

10. Ibid., p. 44.

11. Ibid., pp. 40, 44, 63.

12. Ibid., pp. 6, 41.

13. Ibid., p. 119.

14. Mark Walsh, "Wait Until Law School to Write About the Law, Kagan tells Grassly," *ABA Journal*, June 20, 2010, http://www.abajournal.com/news/article/wait_until_law_school_to_write_about_law_kagan_tells_grassley/.

15. "Harvard Law School History," Harvard Law School, webpage last updated October 2012, http://www.law.harvard.edu/about/history.html.

16. Ibid.

17. Ibid.

18. Charlie Savage and Lisa Faye Petak, "A B-Minus? The Shock! The Horror!," *New York Times*, May 24, 2010, http://www.nytimes.com/2010/05/25/us/politics/25kagan.html?_r=0.

19. Ibid.; Goldstein, Leonnig, and Slevin, "For Supreme Court Nominee Elena Kagan, a History of Pragmatism over Partisanship."

20. Elena Kagan, "Elena Kagan Curriculum Vitae," 2010, http://www.washingtonpost.com/wp-srv/politics/documents/KaganCorrespondence.pdf.

21. Derrick Bell, "The Supreme Court 1984 Term: The Civil Rights Chronicles," *Harvard Law Review*, November 1985, 99. Harv.L.Rev.4, http://www.lexisnexis.com.ezproxy2.rmc.edu/hottopics/lnacademic/?.

22. Ibid.

23. Ibid.

24. Chelsea Rudman, "Brietbart Exclusive: Kagan's Notes on Derrick Bell's Law Review Article were 'Handwritten,'" *Media Matters for America*, April 26, 2012, http://mediamatters.org/blog/2012/04/26/breitbart-exclusive-kagans-notes-on-derrick-bel/185593.

25. John Schwartz, "In a Mentor, Kagan's Critics See Liberal Agenda," *New York Times*, June 25, 2010, http://www.nytimes.com/2010/06/26/us/politics/26mikva.html.

26. Goldstein, Leonnig, and Slevin, "For Supreme Court Nominee Elena Kagan, a History of Pragmatism over Partisanship."

27. Schwartz, "In a Mentor, Kagan's Critics See Liberal Agenda"; Greg Hinz, "Ab Mikva Talks about His Ex-Clerk, Elena Kagan," *Crain's Chicago Business*, May 10, 2010, http://www.chicagobusiness.com/article/20100510/BLOGS02/305109993/ab-mikva-talks-about-his-ex-clerk-elena-kagan.

Chapter 5

THE MAKINGS
OF A LEGAL SCHOLAR

In late February 1986, Supreme Court Justice Thurgood Marshall received the following letter:

Dear Justice Marshall,

I am applying for a judicial clerkship for the 1987 Term. I am currently the Supervising Editor of the *Harvard Law Review* and will spend the coming year clerking for the Honorable Abner J. Mikva of the District of Columbia Circuit.

Enclosed please find a resume, transcript, and writing sample. You will also receive letters of recommendation from Professors Abram Chayes (617–495–xxxx), Frank Michelman (617–495–xxxx), and Charles Nesson (617–495–xxxx) of the Harvard Law School.

Thank you very much for your consideration. I would be honored to serve as your clerk.

Sincerely,

Elena Kagan[1]

Kagan's transcript which accompanied her letter showed that at the time of her graduation from Harvard Law School, she had earned As in 17 of the 21 courses she had taken. Her letters of recommendation all supported her application; in particular, Frank I. Michelman urged Marshall to take Kagan on, despite the two low marks she received her first year in law school. Michelman, who taught Kagan during her first year, argued that Kagan merited the clerkship because of her hard work and dedication to the law. Marshall was apparently convinced for he offered Kagan the clerkship.[2]

CLERKING FOR A GIANT

Clerking for any Supreme Court justice is no small job. On average one thousand law students apply for one of 36 slots every year. Of that number, maybe 200 to 300 applicants are considered serious candidates. To make the cut takes more than excellent grades, outstanding letters of recommendation or an interesting background. It also takes determination and a bit of luck to land one of these coveted positions.

Clerking for Justice Thurgood Marshall would be considered by many law graduates the dream of a lifetime. Marshall, considered one of America's finest legal minds, was also to many to be nothing short of a hero, especially in the field of civil rights. He is also revered by many Americans, both black and white, as part of a trinity that includes the Reverend Martin Luther King, Jr. and Malcolm X. Together, these three men represent three of the most important African American civil rights figures of the late-20th century.

Born on July 2, 1908, in Baltimore, Maryland, Marshall was the son of a steward and a kindergarten teacher. One of his father's favorite pastimes was to listen to court cases at the local courthouse, and then return home to discuss the cases and the lawyers' arguments with his two sons. Marshall later admitted, "Now you want to know how I got involved in law? I don't know. The nearest I can get is that my dad, my brother, and I had the most violent arguments you ever heard about anything. I guess we argued five out of seven nights at the dinner table." Marshall attended Baltimore's Colored High and Training School; he earned a reputation as an above-average student with a flair for talking which made him a star on the school's debate team. Marshall was not

Supreme Court Justice Thurgood Marshall, the first African American appointed to the U.S. Supreme Court. (Joseph Lavenburg, National Geographic Society, Collection of the Supreme Court of the United States)

above mischief-making though; his greatest accomplishment in high school was his memorization of the entire U.S. Constitution, a punishment for misbehaving in class.[3]

After graduating from high school, Marshall was accepted at the all-male Lincoln University in Oxford, Pennsylvania. Settling into school proved a bit difficult; Marshall was suspended twice for his pranks and hazing of other classmates. Marshall's goal ultimately was to study law, but in the beginning he stayed away from local campus politics. However, by his sophomore year, Marshall was participating in a protest against a segregated movie theater. He also began taking his studies more seriously, in part because of the encouragement of his girlfriend, Vivien Bury, who later became his wife. In 1929, Marshall graduated with high honors from Lincoln, with a degree in American literature and philosophy.[4]

It was Marshall's hopes to attend law school at the University of Maryland; however, the school had a strict segregation policy, and so Marshall entered Howard University for his studies. During this time, his views on discrimination were heavily influenced by the dean of the Law School, Charles Hamilton Houston, who believed in the power of the Constitution and its abilities to help all Americans, regardless of race or color. For Houston, the biggest battle ahead was the need to overturn the 1898 Supreme Court ruling *Plessy v. Ferguson*, which established the doctrine of "separate but equal," which in effect banished African Americans to second-class accommodations from schools to seats on a city bus.[5]

Upon his graduation from law school, Marshall took on his first major court case in 1933, when he successfully sued the University of Maryland to admit its first African American student to its law school. The irony was not lost upon Marshall, who had unsuccessfully tried for admission to the school years earlier. Marshall later moved to New York City where he became chief counsel for the NAACP. During this period, he also helped to draft the constitutions of two new emerging African nations: Ghana and what is now modern-day Tanzania. Marshall also won a number of legal victories against segregation, in effect breaking down the color line in the areas of transportation, housing, and voting. But, by far, Marshall's most famous case was the 1954 Supreme Court decision *Brown v. Board*, which struck down state-sponsored discrimination to schools. In all, Marshall won 14 of the 19 cases he argued before the Supreme Court, making him the most successful lawyer to ever argue and win more cases before that court than any other American.[6]

In 1961, President John F. Kennedy appointed Thurgood Marshall to the U.S. Court of Appeals for the Second Circuit. While on the bench, Marshall wrote over 150 decisions that included support for the rights of immigrants, the limiting of government intrusion in cases involving illegal search and seizure, as well as decisions over legal practices of double jeopardy; Marshall also tackled the thorny problem of right to privacy issues. It is a testament to Marshall's brilliant legal mind that none of the 98 majority decisions he wrote while on the Second Circuit Bench was ever reversed by the Supreme Court. In 1965, President Lyndon Johnson appointed Judge Marshall to the office of U.S. Solicitor General; two years later, Marshall became the first African American appointed to the U.S. Supreme Court.[7]

MARSHALL'S NEW LAW CLERK

By 1988, Justice Thurgood Marshall had been sitting on the court bench for almost two decades. The court had undergone a dramatic shift moving from the more liberal Warren Court to a bench headed by William Rehnquist, a far more conservative justice. Marshall was "in his decline and alienated, marginalized" and "looking for really bright people to kind of put a new charge in him" and to help him write dissenting opinions. In hiring Kagan, Marshall hoped to put the spark back in his legal decisions. But Kagan was not clerking for Marshall because she wholeheartedly agreed with his legal views. As political reporter and writer Juan Williams later stated, "She didn't come to him because she was necessarily of like mind, although she was coming out of the same political milieu." If anything, Kagan appeared to have a far more ambivalent attitude toward Marshall and his legal decisions.[8]

Kagan, writing years later in a tribute to Thurgood Marshall, recounted their first meeting:

> I first spoke with Justice Marshall in the summer of 1986, a few months after I had applied to him for a clerkship position. (It seems odd to call him Justice Marshall in these pages. My co-clerks and I called him "Judge" or "Boss" to his face, "TM" behind his back; he called me, to my face and I imagine also behind my back, "Shorty.") He called me one day and, with little in the way of preliminaries, asked me whether I still wanted a job in his chambers. I responded that I would love a job. "What's that?" he said, "you already have a job?" I tried, in every way I could, to correct his apparent misperception. I yelled, I shouted, I screamed that I did not have a job, that I wanted a job, that I would be honored to work for him. To all of which he responded: "Well, I don't know, if you already have a job. . . ." Finally, he took pity on me, assured me that he had been in jest, and confirmed that I would have a job in his chambers. He asked me, as I recall, only one further question: whether I thought I would enjoy working on dissents.[9]

Kagan also remembered Marshall's humility; he had little use for pomposity or pretence. Another of Marshall's clerks described him as:

> down to earth and humble as a man could be. He was not impressed with his . . . exalted position. He treated everyone

exactly the same. That meant he had no less respect and no more respect than he had for the lowest level employee in the building. Equality was not an abstract principle with him; it was a natural instinct.[10]

This emphasis on equality was also demonstrated in one of the first conversations Kagan had with her new boss. When drafting the constitution for the new nation of Kenya, Marshall had the opportunity to meet with Prince Philip of England. The prince began their conversation by saying, "Do you care to hear my opinion on lawyers?" Marshall replied, "Only if you care to hear my opinion of princes."[11]

Whatever differences Kagan may have had with her boss, she also seemed to enjoy a congenial relationship with Marshall. Her nickname while working for Marshall was "Shorty," though he also referred to her as "Little Bits." The "knucklehead" reference was not reserved for Kagan alone; as one of Marshall's clerks stated years later, their boss, when necessary, called all his clerks by that name when displeased. The clerks worked with Marshall in his office, whose décor consisted mainly of books, objects from Africa, red Naugahyde chairs, and graceless desks. Marshall preferred to work in an anteroom to his main office, where he sat in a comfortable chair across a large table from his clerks to discuss cases, or else just regaling his clerks with stories about his life. As one clerk later recalled, "You're at the same time laughing because he's such a great raconteur and also thinking it's unbelievable that these things happened in the lifetime of this person in whose presence I'm sitting, and their life made such a difference in re-creating a South where he had to be out of town by sunset or his life was in danger."[12]

Kagan later wrote of Marshall's storytelling:

The stories were something more than diversions (though, of course, they were that too). They were a way of showing us that, bright young legal whipper-snappers though we were, we did not know everything; indeed, we knew, when it came to matters of real importance, nothing. They were a way of showing us foreign experiences and worlds, and in doing so, of reorienting our perspectives on even what had seemed most familiar. And they served another function as well: they reminded us, as Justice Marshall thought all lawyers (and certainly all judges) should be reminded, that behind law there are stories—stories of people's lives as shaped by law, stories of people's lives as might be changed by law. Justice Marshall had little use for law as abstraction, divorced from social reality . . . his stories kept us focused on law as a source of human well-being.[13]

TAKE A MEMO

One of the primary tasks assigned to the clerks was the writing of brief memorandums evaluating the thousands of cases appealed to the Supreme Court every year. In looking over memorandums written by Kagan during the period 1987–1988, one is allowed a glimpse of one of the few paper trails left behind by Kagan. The memos also offer a window into Kagan's attitudes early in her law career which tended to favor a more liberal sensibility on topics ranging from environmental regulations, rights of property owners to the rights of criminals.

Many of Kagan's memos to Marshall are straightforward in their interpretation; however, some of her comments caution Marshall against hearing a case because of the decided shift to the right that the then-current Supreme Court was taking. Kagan was also concerned over how a ruling might "elevate outcomes over the law." One example was a memo written on October 7, 1987, in which Kagan analyzed the case *United States v. Shonde*, which had been kicked up the U.S. Court of Appeals, Eighth Circuit, in 1986. The case involved a judge dismissing an immigrant's guilty plea over a minor infraction; if the judge had gone ahead with the plea, the immigrant's application for permanent residency would be jeopardized. The Justice Department appealed, stating that the judge had exceeded his authority. Kagan sided with the Justice Department, noting that their view was the correct one. However, she still recommended against the Supreme Court hearing the appeal because the judge in the original case had "ensured an equitable result" at "no great cost to the Republic." Justice Marshall thought otherwise; a scrawled "D" for "deny" was inscribed at the top of Kagan's memo.[14]

In another case, *City of Santa Barbara v. Hall*, Kagan took issue with a court ruling that she found too conservative. In an angry memo, Kagan urged Marshall to overturn an appeals court ruling over the issue of a rent control ordinance. The case began when the owners of a mobile home park challenged a mobile home rent control ordinance enacted by the City of Santa Barbara. The ordinance, aside from setting certain limits on cent increases, provided that a park owner may evict a tenant only for cause. The District Court dismissed the case, but the Circuit Court of Appeals reversed the decision stating that the case must go to trial. The court also suggested that the proper outcome of the case would be the invalidation of the rent control ordinance under the Fifth Amendment.[15]

Kagan's response to the court decision was heated: "All in all, this opinion is outrageous," Kagan wrote to Marshall. In her opinion, the judge "flouted the opinions of this court and has reached a result that is sweeping in its implications. Although the decision does not invalidate the ordinance on its merits, it is an authorization for broad, wholesale attacks on rent control regulation." But both Marshall and the Supreme Court passed on hearing the case and decided to let the ruling stand.[16]

The rent control case memorandum was one of several dozen cases in which Kagan appeared to take a stronger personal interest. Her memos to Marshall were often written with great emotion and at great length. The memorandums also serve to illustrate Kagan's view that the Constitution contained unwritten rights protecting personal liberty—a view often called the "substantive due process doctrine" that the Warren Court applied to a number of famous rulings, such as the 1973 one that struck down state-banned abortions. Critics of this liberal interpretation of the Constitution have charged that, in fact, the substantive due process doctrine did little in terms of a strict interpretation of constitutional law; in reality, the process allowed judges to create new rights as the case merits.[17]

THE RIGHTS OF CHILDREN

The rights of children were the focus of two memos written in the fall of 1987. The first, *Dehaney v. Winnebago County*, was especially trying.

The question in this case was whether a reckless failure by welfare authorities to protect a child from a parent's abuse constituted an abuse of the Fourteenth Amendment. The background of the case was a difficult one; beginning in 1983, a child was brought to the local hospital with bruises and abrasions. The Winnebago County Social Services was contacted and the child was placed in the custody of the hospital. A few days later, a lawyer for a child protective team determined that the child could go home, as there was insufficient evidence of abuse. A month later, the child was back at the hospital with what was described as suspicious injuries. Again, it was determined that there was not enough evidence of child abuse to warrant taking the child away from his father. Over the course of several months, the child was taken to the hospital with suspicious injuries, but each time was sent back home. Finally, a year later, the child was beaten so severely by his father that he fell into a coma and suffered severe brain damage.[18]

A lawsuit was brought against the county and the social worker for failing to take the necessary actions to protect the child. However, the district court saw no case and dismissed the suit. The Court of Circuit Appeals also concurred, stating that while the county had been negligent, negligence alone was not enough reason to take the case to trial. In essence, the court charged that is was not the county's duty to protect the constitutional rights of a child. For Kagan, the lawsuit raised the question as to whether any government agency had an unwritten constitutional duty to help such children. In an emotional three-page memorandum, Kagan outlined the case and then expressed worry that a court majority would use the case as a reason to reject the doctrine of substantive due process, a real concern given the conservative stance of the court. If the court ruled in favor of the county, it would be sending a strong message that the government does not have the right to "affirmatively do things."[19]

A few months later, another case debating the rights of a child was tackled by Kagan. *Ledbetter v. Taylor* centered on the abuse suffered by a child taken into a foster home. The child in question suffered severe injuries at the hands of her foster mother and lapsed into a coma. The Gwinnett County (Georgia) Department of Family and Children Services had placed the child in the foster home. Subsequent to the injuries, the child's guardian filed a suit against state and county officials responsible for placing the child in the foster home. The complaint alleged that in failing to provide adequate inspection and supervision of the foster home, state and county officials acted with deliberate indifference to the child's rights under both the Eighth and Fourteenth Amendments. The suit also charged that the child had been deprived of due process of law.[20]

Initially, the U.S. District Court for the Northern District of Georgia dismissed the complaint for failure to state a claim upon which relief could be granted. At first, the Court of Appeals upheld the decision, but then later reversed itself, stating that state regulations imposed a duty of state officials to insure the safety of children placed in foster care. Kagan, in her memo, wrote that "some members of this court will doubtless object" to an appeals court ruling that the authorities had violated the child's constitutional rights, but she thought it was "correct."[21]

CRIMINAL RIGHTS

Other memorandums written by Kagan dealt with law enforcement issues. In more than a dozen memorandums concerning the rights of prisoners or suspects, written during her time clerking for Marshall, Kagan demonstrated a strategic, yet realistic, tone in trying to stop the increasingly conservative Rehnquist court to roll back liberal precedents concerning the rights of the accused and jailed.

One such instance was the case *Paskins v. Illinois*, in which two men who were walking in an area where a crime had been committed were stopped by a police officer. The officer told the men to approach while holding a gun on them, made the two lie down for five minutes, and then frisked the two. In the meantime, backup was called to aid the officer. The search turned up evidence of a crime. The men wanted the evidence suppressed, arguing that the police had arrested them without probable cause to believe they had committed a crime. A lower court sided with the police, ruling that the five-minute incident did not amount to an arrest, but rather was a brief "stop and frisk" that does not require probable cause. Kagan's sense of outrage was evident in the memo, calling the decision "fairly outrageous," but she also wrote, "I think a defensive denial is in order. I would think that if the Court took this case, it would hold that the conduct here was consistent with the notion of a Terry stop, which would be awful and perhaps quite consequential holding."[22]

In another memorandum, Kagan criticized a lower court ruling in the case *Lanzaro v. Monmouth County Correctional Institution Inmates*, which suggested that the Constitution required a sheriff's office to pay for female inmates to have elective abortions. Kagan's response to Marshall was sharp but thoughtful:

> Quite honestly, I think that although a lot of this decision is well-intentioned, parts of it are ludicrous. Since elective abortions are not medically necessary, I cannot see how denial of such abortions *is* a breach of the Eighth Amendment obligation to provide prisoners with needed medical care. And given that nonprisoners have no rights to funding for abortions, I do not see why prisoners should have such rights. Of course, I recommend that you deny this petition, but I think the Court will probably grant it. Judge Higginbotham simply went *too* far; this case is likely to become the vehicle that this Court uses to create some very bad law on abortion and/or prisoners' rights.[23]

In another case, *Torres v. Oakland Scavenger*, Marshall voted not to let a man pursue a discrimination claim because his lawyer, who was blind, accidentally left his name off an appeal, and a deadline expired. Ms. Kagan and her fellow clerks sought to persuade Justice Marshall to change his vote until he grew annoyed and, pointing to his framed judicial commission on the wall, asked them whose name was on it. Kagan later wrote about this case in her memoriam article on Marshall in 1993:

> The question for the Court was whether the appellate court had jurisdiction over the party whose name had been omitted; on this question rode the continued existence of the employee's discrimination claim. My co-clerks and I pleaded with Justice Marshall to vote (as Justice Brennan eventually did) that the appellate court could exercise jurisdiction. Justice Marshall refused. . . . The Justice referred in our conversation to his own years of trying civil rights claims. All you could hope for, he remarked, was that a

court didn't rule against you for illegitimate reasons; you couldn't hope, and you had no right to expect, that a court would bend the rules in your favor. Indeed, the Justice continued, it was the very existence of rules— along with the judiciary's felt obligation to adhere to them—that best protected unpopular parties. Contrary to some conservative critiques, Justice Marshall believed devoutly—believed in a near-mystical sense—in the rule of law. He had no trouble writing the Torres opinion.[24]

Most of the memorandums written by Kagan are concise and to the point, at times even terse. For example, in the case *Sandidge v. The United States*, Kagan wrote only four sentences in describing the circumstances: a Washington, D.C., resident was challenging the city's strict gun control ordinance on the grounds that he had an individual right to bear arms under the Second Amendment. Although in 2008 the Supreme Court would vote five to four to strike down the city's ordinance because of that very reason, in 1987, Kagan had little use for the suit or the claim, simply writing, "I'm not sympathetic."[25]

KADRMAS v. DICKINSON PUBLIC SCHOOLS, NO. 86–7113

But the case that Marshall most cared about during Kagan's tenure as clerk was a school busing case, *Kadrmas v. Dickinson Public Schools*, in 1988. That spring, Marshall assigned Kagan to write a draft of his opinion on a case; the case concerned whether a school district had the right to charge a family of poor means for busing their child to the nearest school, located 16 miles away. The majority opinion on the court was that the busing fee was, in fact, constitutional. Marshall, however, disagreed strongly with the decision and planned to write a dissenting opinion.[26]

Kagan disagreed with her boss, telling Marshall that it "would be difficult to find in favor of the child" under legal doctrine; Marshall was so incensed at her opinion that he called her a knucklehead. In addition, Marshall gave Kagan back her drafts, criticizing her for "failing to express—or for failing to express in a properly pungent tone—his understanding of the case." When asked why Marshall was so adamant about siding with the family, Kagan later wrote that he had "allowed his personal experiences, and the knowledge of suffering and deprivation gained from those experiences, to guide him."[27]

The final draft seems to implicitly acknowledge that his vote rested less on legal doctrine than on his notion of social justice. The case, it says, asked "whether a state may discriminate against the poor in providing access to education," adding, "I regard this question as one of great urgency. As I have stated on prior occasions, proper analysis of equal protection claims depends less on choosing the formal label under which the claim should be reviewed than upon identifying and carefully analyzing the real interests at stake."[28]

Clearly, there was a crucial difference in attitudes. As one law professor pointed out years later, "Ms. Kagan did not share those experiences. . . . It's absurd to compare Elena Kagan's judicial philosophy to Thurgood Marshall's philosophy. . . . Their times and life experiences are different. They lived in different worlds. The reality is that Elena Kagan learned a lot from Justice Marshall, but she will not be overly influenced by Marshall or anyone else. She is her own person." There were other differences between the two. Marshall believed the death penalty to be unconstitutional while Kagan felt the opposite, stating later, "I am not morally opposed to capital punishment," and that she acknowledged the Court's precedents concerning the death penalty as "constitutional in a wide variety of cases and circumstances."[29]

Years later, Kagan would later distance herself from many of those memos during her 2010 confirmation hearing; saying that her job as Marshall's clerk was simply to channel the justice's mind-set on particular topics. Kagan would also explain that her job as Marshall's clerk was one that simply tried to "facilitate his work, and to enable him to advance his goals and purposes as a justice. . . . He knew what he thought about most issues. And for better or for worse, he was not really interested in engaging with his clerks on first principles." But Kagan also acknowledged her role in the memos. At her confirmation hearings, she stated, "I don't want to say that there is nothing of me in these memos," and "I think that it's actually fair when you look" at a particular memorandum "to think that I was stating an opinion."[30]

That, however, did not diminish the way she felt about Marshall or her brief time clerking for him. Writing about Marshall in 1993, Kagan stated:

> I knew, of course, before I became his clerk that Justice Marshall had been the most important—and probably the greatest—lawyer of the twentieth century. I knew that he had shaped the strategy that led to *Brown v. Board of Education* and other landmark civil rights cases; that he had achieved great renown (indeed, legendary status) as a trial lawyer. . . . But in my year of clerking, I think I saw what had made him great. Even at the age of eighty, his mind was active and acute, and he was an almost instant study. Above all, though, he had the great lawyer's talent (a talent many judges do not possess) for pinpointing a case's critical fact or core issue. That trait, I think, resulted from his understanding of the pragmatic—of the way in which law worked in practice as well as on the books, of the way in which law acted on people's lives. If a clerk wished for a year of spinning ever more refined (and ever less plausible) law-school hypotheticals, she might wish for a clerkship other than Justice Marshall's. If she thought it more important for a Justice to understand what was truly going on in a case and to respond to those realities, she belonged in Justice Marshall's chambers.[31]

NOTES

1. Elena Kagan, "Elena Kagan's Application for Justice Marshall Clerkship," February 19, 1986, http://www.paperlessarchives.com/ElenaKaganDocumentsA22.pdf.

2. Charlie Savage and Lisa Faye Petak, "A B-Minus? The Shock! The Horror!," *New York Times*, May 24, 2010, http://www.nytimes.com/2010/05/25/us/politics/25kagan.html?_r=0.

3. "Thurgood Marshall," Biography.com, n.d., http://www.biography.com/people/thurgood-marshall-9400241?page=1.

4. Juan Williams, "Thurgood Marshall's Early Life," Thurgood Marshall, n.d., http://www.thurgoodmarshall.com/interviews/early_life.htm.

5. "Thurgood Marshall," Biography.com.

6. "Thurgood Marshall," n.d., http://chnm.gmu.edu/courses/122/hill/marshall.htm.

7. Juan Williams, "Thurgood Marshall: American Revolutionary," n.d., http://www.thurgoodmarshall.com/home.htm.

8. Charlie Savage, "Kagan's Link to Marshall Cuts 2 Ways," *New York Times*, May 12, 2010, http://www.nytimes.com/2010/05/13/us/politics/13marshall.html?pagewanted=all.

9. Elena Kagan, "In Memoriam: Thurgood Marshall," *Texas Law Review*, May, 1993—71 Tex. L. Rev. 1125, p. 1125.

10. Todd C. Peppers and Artemus Ward, ed., *In Chambers: Stories of Supreme Court Law Clerks and Their Justices* (Charlottesville: University of Virginia Press, 2012), p. 315.

11. Ibid.

12. Savage, "Kagan's Link to Marshall Cuts 2 Ways."

13. Kagan, "In Memoriam," *Texas Law Review*, May, 1993—71 Tex. L. Rev. 1125, p. 1126.

14. Savage, "Kagan's Link to Marshall Cuts 2 Ways"; *United States v. Shonde*, 803F. 2d 937 Court of Appeals 8th Circuit, 1986, http://scholar.google.com/scholar_case?case=3472359426723034640&hl=en&as_sdt=2&as_vis=1&oi=scholarr.

15. "A Selection of Kagan's Marshall Memos," *New York Times*, June 3, 2010, http://documents.nytimes.com/a-selection-of-kagans-marshall-memos#document/p1.

16. Ibid.

17. Charlie Savage, "In Supreme Court Work, Early Views of Kagan," *New York Times*, June 3, 2010, http://www.nytimes.com/2010/06/04/us/politics/04kagan.html?pagewanted=all&_r=0.

18. *Dehaney v. Winnebago County*, *New York Times*, June 3, 2010, http://documents.nytimes.com/a-selection-of-kagans-marshall-memos#document/p4.

19. *Dehaney v. Winnebago County*, *New York Times*, June 3, 2010, http://documents.nytimes.com/a-selection-of-kagans-marshall-memos#document/p5; Savage, "In Supreme Court Work, Early Views of Kagan."

20. *Ledbetter v. Taylor*, *New York Times*, June 3, 2010, http://documents.nytimes.com/a-selection-of-kagans-marshall-memos#document/p8.

21. *Ledbetter v. Taylor*, *New York Times*, June 3, 2010, http://documents.nytimes.com/a-selection-of-kagans-marshall-memos#document/p9.

22. *Paskins v. Illinois*, *New York Times*, June 3, 2010, http://documents.nytimes.com/a-selection-of-kagans-marshall-memos#document/p10.

23. *Lanzaro v. Monmouth County Correctional Institution Inmates*, *New York Times*, June 3, 2010, http://documents.nytimes.com/a-selection-of-kagans-marshall-memos#document/p10.

24. Savage, "Kagan's Link to Marshall Cuts 2 Ways"; *Torres v. Oakland Scavenger* (1987) http://caselaw.lp.findlaw.com/cgi-bin/getcase.pl?court=us&vol=487&invol=312; Kagan, "In Memoriam," *Texas Law Review*, May, 1993—71 Tex. L. Rev. 1125, p. 1128.

25. Savage, "Kagan's Link to Marshall Cuts 2 Ways"; *Sandidge v. The United States*, *New York Times*, June 3, 2010, http://documents.nytimes.com/a-selection-of-kagans-marshall-memos#document/p4.

26. Savage, "Kagan's Link to Marshall Cuts 2 Ways."

27. Ibid.

28. Ibid.

29. Ibid.

30. Ibid.; Savage, "In Supreme Court Work, Early Views of Kagan."

31. Kagan, "In Memoriam," *Texas Law Review*, May, 1993—71 Tex. L. Rev. 1125, pp. 1128–9.

Chapter 6

PRACTICING AND TEACHING

Kagan's clerkship with Thurmond Marshall ended in late 1988. By early 1989, Kagan had found another position, this time as a junior associate at the prestigious law firm Williams & Connolly, also located in Washington, D.C. For the next two years, Kagan would continue her legal education, as she branched out into other areas of the law while working at the firm. Her time with Williams & Connolly also highlights Kagan's willingness to work as part of a team, and her sturdy work ethic.

THE FIRM

Williams & Connolly has a distinguished pedigree. The firm was founded in 1967 by Edward Bennett Williams, recognized as one of the greatest trial lawyers of the late 20th century. Williams was known for his courtroom oratory, his mastery of cross-examination, a seasoned writer of legal briefs, and for his tireless preparations to bring a case to trial. Williams, although moving in the circles of the powerful and wealthy in Washington, was also a champion of unpopular and seemingly unwinnable causes. Williams partnered with a former student at Georgetown, Paul Connolly, to establish Williams & Connolly. From its early beginnings, the two men set out to practice law with a passion and also with what Williams called "contest living" or "embracing the competition and fighting relentlessly to win."[1]

Early on, Williams & Connolly distinguished itself from other white shoe law firms in Washington D.C. For one, the entire firm— all 275 lawyers—was housed in the same building located on Twelfth Street NW. For another, in the last 25 years, all of the firm's partners with one exception were trained and promoted within the firm, a feat not often seen in large law firms anywhere. The firm's primary focus was litigation and it handled cases all over the world from its single office. The firm's corporate clients include major global companies from virtually every industry, including ADM, General Electric, Pfizer, Sony, Sprint Nextel, and UBS. The firm has also taken on numerous law firms and accounting firms in professional responsibility and other litigation earning the firm the reputation that it is Williams & Connolly other firms "turn to when they're in trouble."[2]

At first, the law firm's cases focused on defending individuals in criminal and civil matters; among their more famous clients was Oliver North, who was being investigated by Congress over his role in the Iran-Contra scandal in 1986. Former president Bill Clinton was another high-profile client; the firm represented him during his impeachment trial in 1998. In 2008, Williams & Connolly represented the late Senator Ted Stevens at his trial on charges of making false statements.[3]

In addition to criminal cases, Williams & Connolly was also known for handling "bet-the-company" civil litigation—that is, trials which involved high stakes and complex litigation over such situations as securities law, intellectual property, mass torts, and products liabilities. Another facet of the firm is its intellectual property practice, which has successfully defended patents protecting products with hundreds of millions of dollars in annual sales. Williams & Connolly has presented oral arguments in front of the Supreme Court five times in four years.[4]

Beyond litigation, the firm also assists companies, chief executives, authors, news correspondents, and sports figures in contract matters. Their client list reads like a Who's Who of American celebrities, including President Barack Obama; former presidents Bill Clinton and George W. Bush; Secretary of State Hillary Rodham Clinton; former British prime minister Tony Blair; the late Senator Ted Kennedy; former Federal Reserve chair Alan Greenspan; First Lady Michelle Obama; NBC news anchor Brian Williams; and NBA players Grant Hill, Tim Duncan, Ray Allen, and Shane Battier.[5]

Williams & Connolly has also been ranked as the best law firm to work for in the country, as well as the best firm for white-collar criminal defense and third for general commercial litigation. Former lawyers at the firm have also distinguished themselves in other areas, including serving on the bench of the federal courts, as high-level government officials, as well as top executives and general counsels of major global companies.[6]

ELENA KAGAN, JUNIOR ASSOCIATE

During her confirmation hearings for Solicitor General in 1999, Kagan remarked of her brief time in private practice that "I suspect that a number of the opposing counsel will not remember me." Although Kagan's time with Williams & Connolly was relatively brief—her time at the firm spanned only two years—her record of cases does merit close inspection. It not only would shape her future academic career in the law, but it also put her in the midst of some dramatic and colorful clients, including the rap group 2 Live Crew, the tabloid newspaper *National Enquirer*, and James "The Amazing" Randi, a magician and self-proclaimed professional skeptic.[7]

As a junior associate, Kagan had a number of responsibilities, including drafting briefs and conducting discovery, which meant looking at evidence in preparation for trial. In one instance, Kagan tracked a grand jury investigation. She also argued several cases before judges. Judge Abner J. Mikva, whom Kagan had worked under, stated in a later interview that Kagan "felt it was a part of her training, something she had to do. . . . It may not have been the most fun thing for her, but she did it well." Although Kagan was never in charge of a case, she was associated with the firm's more prominent lawyers. However, one aspect Kagan did not do much of was pro bono work; she would later opt to serve on nonprofit boards.[8]

NOTABLE CASES

During the short time Kagan worked at Williams & Connolly, she did become involved in several high-profile legal cases, handling at least five lawsuits that involved First Amendment or media law issues and libel issues. In three of these cases, Kagan's role was significant; the cases included the representation of a publishing company in a libel action arising from an allegation that the plaintiff was in prison for child molestation, the representation of *Newsweek* in a matter where the plaintiff claimed he had been defamed by being identified as a sub-ject of a fraud investigation, and the representation of the *National Enquirer* in a libel action brought by a person mistakenly identified in the publication. Each of these cases tested Kagan's knowledge with the legal standards applied in libel cases, such as the actual malice standard, which constitutes malice in a libel suit, and the libel-proof plaintiff doctrine, i.e. plaintiffs who appear to be safeguarded from libel actions and suits.[9]

OBSCENITY

In 1989, Kagan gained familiarity with the obscenity standard, when Williams & Connolly took on the high-profile obscenity case against the hip hop group 2 Live Crew. Earlier that summer, U.S. District Court Judge Jose Gonzalez of Fort Lauderdale, Florida, had declared the group's album *As Nasty as They Wanna Be* obscene in the three counties under his jurisdiction. Gonzalez's pronouncement was a first; a Federal court had never before deemed a recording obscene. Adding to the controversy, a record store owner who defied the judge's order and continued to sell the album was arrested. Not long afterward, two members of 2 Live Crew were also arrested for performing their songs before an adults-only audience in Florida. If convicted, they faced hearty fines and a possible prison sentence.[10]

For the trial, the defense attorneys for 2 Live Crew called three ex-pert witnesses to explain the origins and meaning of rap music, arguing that a more complete understanding of the history and culture from which rap emerged would show it to be anything but obscene. The witnesses included John Leland, a music critic for *Newsday*, who was considered an expert on hip hop and rap, and Henry Louis Gates, a noted professor of African American studies, who had written about the place of rap music in African American culture.[11]

Bruce Rogow, an attorney representing the group stated in an interview that he had asked the Recording Industry Association of America to file a friend-of-the-court brief. The association agreed and hired Williams & Connolly. It was up to Kagan to draft the brief. She later explained that in preparing the legal document she hoped to show the "difficulty of finding music obscene under prevailing constitutional law." In 1992, a three-judge panel of the 11th U.S. Circuit Court of Appeals unanimously threw out the trial judge's decision. Rogow later stated of Kagan's work, "It was nicely done, and it was certainly helpful." At her confirmation hearings, Kagan would also emphasize that the 2 Live Crew case was one of the 10 most significant matters she'd handled during her brief practice in private law. This case as well as four others which involved media clients also foreshadowed Kagan's later focus in her academic career on the First Amendment.[12]

In 2010, at the time of Kagan's confirmation hearings, Luther Campbell, a member of 2 Live Crew wrote a column for the *Miami New Times* about why Kagan should be appointed to the Supreme Court. Campbell stated that "My homegirl Kagan was saying people could not be aroused by the lyrics. . . . She did a great job fighting on 2 Live Crew's behalf, which lets you know that Kagan is not easily swayed by public opinion or by politicians with their own hidden agendas. She is not going to let any person or group tell her what is right or wrong."[13]

REPORTER'S PRIVILEGE

The issue of a reporter's privilege with a group of *Washington Post* reporters was another case in which Kagan assisted. Years later, in a *Harvard Law Bulletin* interview, Kagan reflected that the *Post*'s legal strategy to invalidate subpoenas grew from former editor Ben Bradlee's assertion that a reporter's privilege (i.e., the right by reporters to refuse to testify or to be forced to reveal their sources) exists whether the Supreme Court says it does or not. Kagan also stated her surprise that such boilerplate motions to overturn subpoenas had such value in court. As she described it, "[W]hat was shocking is that sometimes we won notwithstanding that there wasn't a whole lot of law in these motions. The prosecutors would back down often after we convinced them that the reporter didn't know anything or wouldn't say anything particularly useful. Or the judge would rule for us on the ground that there wasn't any necessity for the reporter's testimony. And the client—the reporter—never, ever ended up in jail."[14]

But Kagan also realized that there was a possibility of the Supreme Court revisiting the issue, though she stated that the existing situation was not as bad as some made it out to be. As she told the interviewer:

> It's hard to think of important prosecutions that have not gone forward because reporters have refused to give information. On the other hand, it's hard to make the argument that freedom of the press has been terribly infringed by the legal regime that's been set up. So it may be that the Supreme Court looks at the status quo and says: "Nothing seems terribly wrong with this. People are ignoring a little bit what we said, but it seems to have results that are not too bad, from either perspective."[15]

Kagan also recognized the potential problems with a proposed shield law, particularly in deciding who the law would protect, such as bloggers. She pointed out that if such a shield law protected anyone who considered themselves a journalist that "once that happens, there's a real problem for prosecutors seeking to obtain information." At the same time, Kagan recognized the complexity of the First Amendment which may have been one reason why the Supreme Court had chosen not to differentiate between the different types of media and journalism, stating, "First Amendment law is already very complicated . . . [t]here are lots and lots of different kinds of press entities and other speakers. And if each one gets its own First Amendment doctrine, that might be a world we don't want to live in."[16]

COURT ACCESS

Another area of the law that Kagan also worked on involved having open access to court documents. In a case known as *In re Application of News World Communications, Inc.*, Kagan represented the *Washington Post* and a local NBC affiliate who were fighting to have the public release of the unredacted transcripts of audiotapes used as evidence in a criminal trial. The issue at stake was whether or not the public had a right to the information versus the right of a defendant to a fair trial which could be compromised if the documents were released. Kagan argued two motions before Judge Charles Richey of the U.S. District Court in Washington, D.C., in which she asked for the release of the transcripts and that the transcripts not be redacted or edited. The judge granted both motions.[17]

LIBEL CASES

Sometimes, Kagan had a higher profile in a legal case, such as the dispute between the magician and scientific skeptic known as "The Amazing Randi" against Eldon Byrd, an associate of noted psychic Uri Geller, whom Randi had previously accused of being a charlatan. In 1988, in a magazine story published in the *Twilight Zone Magazine*, Randi stated that Byrd, who'd been put on probation for distributing sexually explicit material, was also a child molester. Byrd sued for libel, naming Randi and the magazine publisher, Montcalm Publishing, in his suit. Williams & Connolly represented the publisher; Kagan's job was to draft motions and then argue them before a trial judge in Baltimore where the trial was taking place.

Again, Kagan stressed broad First Amendment principles arguing that an individual's reputation was already tainted (in this case Byrd's pornography conviction) enough to be libel-proof. The case dragged on until 1993, when a jury found Randi guilty of defamation of character, but then did not award Byrd any damages. By then, Elena Kagan had moved on—this time to Chicago and the University of Chicago Law School, where she accepted a position as an associate professor of law.[18]

CHICAGO

The University of Chicago was granted its charter in 1890; two years later, the institution held its first classes. The school had a number of generous donors, including John D. Rockefeller which helped William Rainey Harper, who served as the school's first president, to work toward making the institution one of the nation's finest. It was Harper's dream that the University of Chicago be a true university that not only offered a solid foundation in the liberal arts, but also emphasized advanced training and research.[19]

In 1902, the University of Chicago opened the doors to its new law school. For Harper and the law school faculty, the new program offered an opportunity to offer students a different kind of legal education, one that stressed not only professionalism, but with a much broader out-look than was usually taught at the nation's leading schools of law. For Harper, the university setting offered an education in law that

> implies a scientific knowledge of law and of legal and juristic methods. These are the crystallization of ages of human prog-ress. They cannot be understood in their entirety without a clear comprehension of the historic forces of which they are the prod-uct, and of the social environment with which they are in living contact. A scientific study of law involves the related sciences of history, economics, philosophy—the whole field of man as social being.[20]

This bold approach envisioned by President Harper resulted in the University of Chicago Law School playing a groundbreaking role in the nation's training of its lawyers. The Law School was instrumental in implementing a number of innovations in legal education during the last century, which included: the recognition of new disciplines of law, such as administrative law, legislation, and comparative law, introducing other disciplines into the curriculum, as well as appointing faculty members who were not lawyers. The school also extended legal research to include not only the rules of law but also to "empirically oriented investigations" of the legal system as well as broadening the curriculum to include clinical as well as academic offerings.[21]

KAGAN'S LIFE IN CHICAGO

At the age of 31, Kagan began her new life as an academic in Chicago. For the next four years, she lived in a vintage building in Lincoln Park. As a professor, Kagan seemed to have found her niche. As one former colleague described her, Kagan "wasn't someone who just wanted to go into academics to play with ideas in a more abstruse way. . . . She was interested in real-world institutions and issues." Another friend found Kagan as a scholar to be more "comfortable examining something and analyzing something given to her, and she'll be brilliant at it, and she will see it from different angles. . . . She really is a deep intellectual. . . . She is not married. And although she has many friends, the world of books and ideas is her world."[22]

The former provost of the university law school found Kagan to have great depth as well. In a press release in May 2010, he stated, "Elena quickly established herself as a brilliant teacher, focusing particularly in the areas of constitutional and administrative law. . . . In the classroom, she was tough, sharp, and incisive. The students loved her classes." Another professor found that Kagan "proved herself to be an extraordinary teacher, a very promising scholar and an exceptionally important member of our academic community. Most of all, she was a lawyer's lawyer and a true role model for our students." Another colleague concurred: "Elena quickly established herself as a brilliant teacher, focusing particularly in the areas of constitutional and administrative law. . . . In the classroom, she was tough, sharp and incisive. . . . Elena displayed terrific legal skills as a scholar as well as a teacher. Writing primarily about the First Amendment, she was precise, analytical and insightful in her scholarship. Students of that era will surely recall Elena as one of the best teachers at an institution that prides itself on excellence in teaching."[23]

Students taking her classes found her to be a receptive and excellent teacher. "She was an amazing teacher. She was my favorite," said Carolyn Shapiro, a former student and now a professor at Chicago-Kent College of Law. "She was just unbelievably charismatic in the classroom." Former student Jesse Ruiz, now chairman of the state Board of Education, remembers Kagan as "a really good professor, really concerned about teaching." Kagan often brought students to lunch and dinner; one of her favorite spots was a tapas eatery Cafe Ba BaReeba at 2024 N. Halsted. Students thought so much of her that Kagan was chosen as teacher of the year. Still Kagan craved her alone time; after classes were done for the day, Kagan would get in her car, crank up the radio, and drive home as fast as she could.[24]

*Elena Kagan chatting with former law students on the Harvard campus in 2003.
(AP Photo/Elise Amendola)*

Kagan was very involved in student and faculty activities too. For instance, she played in faculty-student softball games. Kagan was also a star of the faculty trivia team, much to the chagrin of the student team that went up against her. She also showed herself to be a devoted Chicago White Sox fan and would go to as many games as she could. Kagan also was a regular in a long-standing law school tradition of the faculty lunch at the Quadrangle Club at 57th and University. Three times a week, the club hosts a round table which could consist of up to 15 law school faculty members. There was only one rule at the lunch: the conversation was limited to two topics—law or politics. Colleagues found Kagan to be "very lively and opinionated" at the get-togethers.[25]

Still, almost from the beginning, there were those on the faculty who questioned whether Kagan was suited for the life of an academic. Part of the rigors of the job included research and publishing, which was not only important for the school, but also played a large role in whether a professor would receive tenure. Kagan did publish several articles and won tenure in 1995; still, many thought her scholarly output was lean.[26]

MEETING A FUTURE PRESIDENT

Not long after Kagan began teaching at the Law School, she crossed paths with a young man also teaching classes. His name was Barack Obama and he had been recently hired as a lecturer at the law school. While Kagan was a full-time professor, on a tenure track, Obama was working roughly 10 hours a week at the school. While the two did not become close friends, they did spend time with each other as Obama and Kagan often shared common outlooks on politics and law. A former law professor saw the two as "lawyers' lawyers," in that their approach tended toward "here's a legal problem—let's see if I can solve it."[27]

Over time, Obama developed a reputation in the classroom for being a nonpartisan lecturer; and was noted for expanding the legal views of his students. His speaking skills and ability to communicate quickly made him a sought after teacher. As one former student later commented, "I liked that he included both jurisprudence and real politics in class discussions. Lots of classes in law school tend to be judge-centric and had as much a focus on the legislative branch as the judicial branch. That was refreshing."[28]

Students and faculty alike soon recognized that the newcomer had a bright future. Obama had an already established reputation as a fine scholar; among his many accomplishments was serving as the first African American president of the *Harvard Law Review*. Still, given the heady atmosphere of the school where the likes of Elena Kagan, Judge Abner Mikva (Kagan's mentor), and other notable professors of law, Obama had his work cut out for him in standing out among many sterling legal minds.[29]

LEGAL WRITINGS

During her time at Chicago, Kagan published six scholarly law review articles which included topics on First Amendment doctrine and administrative law. In addition, Kagan also published numerous book reviews, encyclopedia entries, and tributes to figures in the law, including a memoriam article for Thurgood Marshall as well as a controversial article on confirmation hearings for nominees for the Supreme Court.

After leaving private practice for academia, Kagan applied a more academic approach to legal areas that she had worked in. One example of this was libel law, as seen in her article "Libel and the First Amendment" for the second edition of the *Encyclopedia of the American Constitution*. In her article, Kagan expressed surprise at how little reform had been undertaken in the wake of the 1964 Supreme Court case *New York Times v. Sullivan*, which established the actual malice standard that is to be met before press reports about public officials or public figures can be considered to be defamatory or libelous. Among the problems Kagan described with libel law is the complexity of case law about libel and how speech is categorized between that of public and private figures. More alarming to Kagan was the fact that the libel law was in conflict with broader First Amendment theory, writing, "The intricate, even convoluted nature of this categorical scheme, governing as it does every important aspect of libel litigation, ill comports with the Court's usual concern for certainty and predictability in matters affecting freedom of speech." Kagan was also skeptical that "actual malice" in public figure cases "deprives falsely defamed individuals of the ability to obtain monetary damages" and "prevents the public from ever learning of the falsity of widely disseminated libelous statements."[30]

Perhaps one of her most well-known papers was "Private Speech, Public Purpose: The Role of Governmental Motive in First Amendment Doctrine," published in 1996 in the *University of Chicago Law Review*. In the article, Kagan argued that the primary purpose of courts charged with reviewing speech restrictions should be clear in finding out impermissible governmental motives, but not necessarily to protect individual expression or the marketplace of ideas. The article also cites arguments Kagan made in two earlier papers concerning a 1992 Supreme Court's 1992 decision in *R.A.V. v. St. Paul*. The decision struck down a city ordinance banning certain bias-motivated conduct, including speech. In one paper, Kagan argued that when government is under no imperative to prohibit or endorse *any* speech, it cannot selectively do so based on the viewpoint of that speech. In the other article, Kagan stated that the Supreme Court can still regulate pornography and hate speech under her interpretation of the First Amendment.[31]

A 2001 article "Presidential Administration," published in the *Harvard Law Review*, was named the year's top scholarly article by the American Bar Association's Section on Administrative Law and Regulatory Practice. In this article, Kagan wrote about an "era of presidential administration," and how the three previous presidents exercised increasingly direct authority over federal agencies. One interesting excerpt of the article is her contention that then-President Bill Clinton "unlike his de-regulatory predecessors" advanced his own progressive and pro-regulatory political agenda.

THE GINSBERG CONFIRMATION

Early in her legal career, Kagan served as a special counsel for then-Senator Joe Biden at the Senate Judiciary Committee, during the Ruth Bader Ginsburg confirmation hearings in 1993. Two years later, Kagan's experience was the subject of a law review article she wrote daring senators to ask tough questions of nominees. In a 1995 review of Stephen Carter's book on confirmation hearings, "Confirmation Messes, Old and New," Kagan took to task senators on the committee for "failing to ask, and nominees for refusing to answer" questions about their views on specific issues. According to Kagan, it was the responsibility of senators to dig hard and deep for information, to ask the hard questions about both a nominee's judicial philosophy, and substantive views on constitutional issues. Nominees should be asked about their views on particular issues that the Court regularly faces, such as "privacy rights, free speech, race and gender discrimination, and so forth." On this view, a nominee ought to refrain only from expressing a "settled intent" to vote a particular way on a particular case that they might hear on the bench.[32]

What makes the article notable is her incisive and cheeky attitude as to how confirmation hearings really do work. Kagan's caustic observations about the qualifications and legal thinking of four members of the court would come back to haunt her at her own confirmation hearings in 2010. In addition, Kagan also discussed her ideas about the role an individual justice's values play in hearing and deciding cases, while arguing that a nominee's lack of judicial experience ought not matter.

Among Kagan's more trenchant observations:

- The Senate would have confirmed Justice Clarence Thomas without too much trouble in 1991 even though "his substantive testimony had become a national laughingstock." The reasons he faced a fight and only barely made it onto the court, by a vote of 52–48, Ms. Kagan wrote, were "the weakness of Justice Thomas's objective qualifications and the later charges of sexual harassment."
- According to Kagan, a nominee's lack of experience on the appellate court should not in any way hinder their confirmation, "if the candidate can demonstrate the requisite intelligence and legal ability through academic scholarship, the practice of law or governmental service of some other kind. . . ."
- Today's confirmation hearings are for the most part "stylized, hollow and all but worthless. The moment at which the public might briefly pause to consider a nominee's conception of the Constitution," she wrote, had degenerated into "a repetition of platitudes." Further, Kagan called on the Senate to hold close "the essential rightness—the legitimacy and the desirability—of exploring a Supreme Court nominee's set of constitutional views and commitments."
- In describing Ruth Bader Ginsburg's technique for answering questions, Kagan noted that "Justice Ginsburg's favored technique took the form of a pincer movement." That is, if a question was too specific, Ginsburg would decline to answer on the grounds that she did not want to predict a potential vote. If the question was too general, the future Justice stated a judge should not deal in abstractions or hypothetical questions. According to Kagan questions that were deemed too specific constituted "anything that might have some bearing on a case that might someday come before the court." She also described what had been too general: "Roughly, anything else worthy of mention."[33]

By 1995, Kagan had won tenure on the basis of a single article in the publication *The Supreme Court Review*, a scholarly journal edited by the

University of Chicago Law School's own faculty as well as a short essay. But change was in the air for Kagan; soon after, her mentor, Abner Mikva would leave the campus to make his way to Washington, D.C. and the Clinton White House. And if he could, he intended to bring Elena Kagan into the fold, not as a policy person, but as a lawyer.

NOTES

1. "History," Williams & Connolly LLC website, 2013, http://www.wc.com/about-history.html.

2. "Firm Overview," Williams & Connolly LLC website, 2013, http://www.wc.com/about.html.

3. Ibid.

4. Ibid.

5. Ibid.

6. Ibid.

7. Michael Doyle, "Kagan's Courtroom Career Includes Brushes with Rappers," May 13, 2010, http://www.mcclatchydc.com/2010/05/13/94119/kagans-courtroom-career-includes.html#.UZKUu6KcHwM.

8. Ibid.

9. The Reporters Committee for Freedom of the Press, "Elena Kagan: Supreme Court Nominee Has Taken Doctrinal Approach to Free-Speech and Free-Press Issues," *News Media & The Law*, Spring 2010, p. 21.

10. Jon Pareles, "An Album is Judged Obscene; Rap: Slick, Violent, Nasty and, Maybe Hopeful," *New York Times*, June 17, 1990, Section 4, 1.

11. Ibid.

12. Doyle, "Kagan's Courtroom Career Includes Brushes with Rappers."

13. Daniel Kreps, "Why the Once-Controversial Rap Group is Throwing Its Support Behind the Supreme Court Justice Nominee," *Rolling Stone*, July 8, 2010, http://www.rollingstone.com/music/news/elena-kagans-biggest-supporter-2-live-crew-20100708.

14. Michael Doyle, "Kagan's Courtroom Career Includes Brushes with Rappers."

15. Ibid.

16. The Reporters Committee for Freedom of the Press, "Elena Kagan."

17. Ibid.

18. Doyle, "Kagan's Courtroom Career Includes Brushes with Rappers."

19. "History of the Law School," University of Chicago Law School, n.d., http://www.law.uchicago.edu/school/history.

20. Ibid.

21. Ibid.

22. Amy Goldstein, Carol D. Leonnig, and Peter Slevin, "For Supreme Court Nominee Elena Kagan, a History of Pragmatism over Partisanship," *Washington Post*, May 11, 2010, http://www.washingtonpost .com/wp-dyn/content/article/2010/05/10/AR2010051002787.html? sid=ST2010080505264.

23. Sarah Galer, "Former Professor Elena Kagan Nominated to Supreme Court," *University of Chicago News Office*, May 10, 2010, http:// www.law.uchicago.edu/node/2998.

24. Lynn Sweet, "Elena Kagan's Chicago Ties: Met Obama at U. of C.; Lived in Lincoln Park," *Chicago Sun-Times*, May 11, 2010, http:// blogs.suntimes.com/sweet/2010/05/elena_kagans_chicago_ties_met. html; CrystakTsoi, "Former Chicago Colleagues Call Kagan 'Tough,' 'Non-Ideological,'" *Chicago Maroon*, May 11, 2010, http://chicagomar oon.com/2010/05/11/obama-taps-former-professor-elena-kagan-for-supreme-court/.

25. Sweet, "Elena Kagan's Chicago Ties."

26. Christi Parsons, "U. of C. Law Faculty Didn't Back Kagan: No Job Offer When She Sought Return after Clinton Duty," *Chicago Tribune*, May 30, 2010, http://articles.chicagotribune.com/2010–05–30/ news/ct-met-kagan-chicago-20100530_1_harvard-law-school-elena-kagan-faculty.

27. Susan Milligan, "Personal Ties Bind Obama, Kagan," *Boston Globe*, May 16, 2010, http://www.boston.com/news/nation/washington/ articles/2010/05/16/personal_ties_bind_obama_kagan/.

28. Robin I. Mordfin, "From the Green Lounge to the White House," University of Chicago Law School, n.d., http://www.law.uchicago.edu/ alumni/magazine/spring09/greenloungetowhitehouse.

29. Ibid.

30. Doyle, "Kagan's Courtroom Career Includes Brushes with Rappers."

31. Ibid.

32. Sweet, "Elena Kagan's Chicago Ties"; Elena Kagan, "Confirmation Messes, Old and New," 62 *University of Chicago Law Review*, 919, 1995, pp. 934–36; Doyle, "Kagan's Courtroom Career Includes Brushes with Rappers."

33. Adam Liptak, "Kagan's View of the Court Confirmation Process, Before She Was a Part of It," *New York Times*, May 11, 2010, http://www.nytimes.com/2010/05/12/us/politics/12court.html?pagewanted=all.

Chapter 7

AT THE WHITE HOUSE

In 1995, Kagan made the decision to leave the University of Chicago. Her reason? An opportunity to work as associate counsel for newly elected president Bill Clinton. Over the course of the next four years, Kagan would serve in a variety of roles in the Clinton administration, including Associate White House Counsel, Deputy Assistant to the President for Domestic Policy, and Deputy Director of the Domestic Policy Council. During this time, Kagan helped craft White House policy on a wide range of issues. Still, leaving was a gamble; although the university allowed Kagan to leave for two years, it was understood she would return or else she would be forced to resign and give up tenure.

WHITE HOUSE COUNSEL

Kagan's appointment came about again through the efforts of her mentor Abner Mikva, who had also been lured away from the University of Chicago by the Clinton administration to serve as chief counsel. Mikva suggested Kagan for the post of associate counsel; once

more, Kagan joined Mikva; together the two crafted executive or-
ders on welfare reform, child support enforcement, and other domestic policy issues. Kagan also worked on some of the thornier issues
that plagued the Clinton White House, including the Whitewater
Controversy, a series of real estate deals that involved the Clintons,
and "Travelgate," another controversy over the White House travel
office.[1]

Years later, the former president recalled the very first presenta-
tion that Kagan made in the Oval office. In late 1995, Clinton was
considering vetoing new legislation that would put a halt to frivolous lawsuits against the securities industry. However, his economic
team and the top Democrats in Congress were opposed to Clinton's
decision to veto the measure. Clinton then asked Kagan to analyze
the pending bill; her recommendation was that the bill would make
it difficult for shareholders to pursue legitimate fraud claims. As
Clinton later stated, "There she was, in her mid-30s starting out in
her career, with the entire economic team, all of them against her
position, and she knew it. . . . She stood there and defended her
conclusion. . . . It was very impressive. She was composed, direct
and totally unfazed that all those guys wanted a different outcome."
In the end, Clinton accepted Kagan's judgment and issued a surprise
veto to the bill.[2]

Kagan had little trouble navigating the politically volatile issues
she faced as an associate counsel for the White House. Such hot-
button topics as abortion, immigration, and religious freedom were
all dealt with a sharp eye and savvy legal approach by Kagan. Up
until her confirmation hearings, many people had assumed that Kagan's role in the Clinton White House to be confined to helping
draft legal policy for the president. However, documents released by
the Clinton Library prior to Kagan's confirmation hearings for the
Supreme Court in 2010 show Kagan as more heavily involved in
White House affairs as was previously thought., The documentation
also outlines her role more clearly in vetting policy matters for the
President.[3]

In viewing the outlines, emails, and notes during this period, it is
difficult to gauge how much of the material reflects Kagan's own views
or whether she was simply adhering to President Clinton's views on

certain issues. Still, these materials offer another look at Kagan's legal thinking. For instance, in 1996, the debate over the medical procedure known as partial-birth abortion, the president outlined four options that would provide an alternative to the then Republican-sponsored legislation. However, Clinton focused on one option that would ban partial-birth abortions even before the fetus was viable except to avert death or serious health consequences for the woman. Kagan in a note to her boss, Jack Quinn, stated that it appeared that Clinton only favored this option above any others.[4]

Kagan pointed out that by pushing for this plan, the White House would be undermining the landmark Supreme Court ruling *Roe v. Wade* which established a woman's right to an abortion before viability. Kagan noted, "The problem with this approach is twofold. . . . First, it is unconstitutional . . . second, the groups will go crazy." Kagan also noted that any bill would have to have a "health exception" to be considered constitutional. She then suggested that two of the other options being considered would be more likely to find favor.[5]

Elena Kagan working with staff and advisors on President Bill Clinton's State of the Union speech at the White House in 1999. (AP Photo/Clinton Presidential Library)

IMMIGRATION

Another problematic topic facing the White House was immigration. At issue was a New York City lawsuit that challenged a federal law which allowed city employees to report illegal immigrants even though local law forbade it. By 1996, Mayor Rudy Giuliani had enacted a "sanctuary city" policy that forbade city employees from contacting the Immigration and Naturalization Service about immigration violations; Giuliani believed that illegal immigrants had the right to send their children to school as well as feeling safe in reporting crime and/or other violations without fear of deportation. That same year, Giuliani sued the federal government over a new federal law, the Illegal Immigration Reform and Immigrant Responsibility Act of 1996. The new law overturned the 1985 executive order by then mayor Ed Koch that barred government employees from turning in illegal immigrants who were trying to get government benefits from the city.[6]

Giuliani ordered city attorneys to defend this policy in federal court, claiming that the new federal law violated the Tenth Amendment—which provided that powers not granted to the federal government by the Constitution, nor prohibited to the states, are reserved to the states or the people. Kagan called the mayor's suit "nearly frivolous" and wrote that "the federal government has strong institutional interests at stake in defending against such 10th Amendment claims." A federal appeals court affirmed dismissal of the suit in 1999.[7]

Kagan was also careful in her advice as to when the White House needed to take a stand and when to back off. When an appeals court struck down a 1988 Arizona constitutional amendment mandating that state officials use only English in documents and state business, Kagan strongly suggested that the administration stay out of the case, noting that some thought the ruling was "extremely expansive and very possibly wrong." She continued, "All in all, it seems that the best course here is to do nothing. From a political standpoint, we don't want to highlight this issue. From a legal standpoint, we don't want to defend the Ninth Circuit's decision."[8]

RELIGIOUS FREEDOM

In the area of religious freedom, Kagan recommended that the government intervene to support religious freedom. In the case, a California court had held that housing discrimination laws prevented a land-lord from refusing to rent to a couple based on marital status. The landlord claimed that her refusal to rent to an unmarried couple was based on her religious opposition to sex outside marriage. Kagan be-lieved that the antidiscrimination statute in question stifled the landlord's religious freedom, and she urged the solicitor general to weigh in on the side of the landlord in the case. Further, Kagan ridiculed the California court decision which stated that the land-lord's religious freedom was not threatened as she could get an-other job. Kagan wrote, "The plurality's reasoning seem to me quite outrageous—almost as if a court were to hold that a state law does not impose a substantial burden on religion because the complainant is free to move to another state." Further, Kagan noted in a memo to her boss Jack Quinn, "[G]iven the importance of this issue to the President and the danger this decision poses to [the Religious Freedom Restoration Act's] guarantee of religious freedom in the State of Cali-fornia, I think there is an argument to be made for urging the Court to review and reverse the decision."[9]

WHITEWATER

Kagan proved invaluable as the president battled a series of scandals throughout his time in office. Two of the most contentious of these matters—Whitewater and a sexual harassment lawsuit brought against the president by Paula Jones—found Kagan in the midst of crafting legal policy to defend the president. In both cases, Kagan was part of an effort by White House aides and staff to mount a defense on the importance of secrecy surrounding presidential deliberations.

The Whitewater case focused on a series of questionable real es-tate deals that involved the Clintons with business partners James and Susan McDougal. In 1978, then Arkansas attorney general Bill Clinton and his wife, Hillary, formed a partnership with the McDougals to bor-row $203,000 to buy 220 acres of land in Arkansas' Ozark Mountains. The two couples then formed the Whitewater Development Corp., in-tending to build vacation homes. During the next several years, Jim McDougal asked the Clintons for checks for various interest payments on the loan or other expenses; the Clintons have repeatedly stated that they were passive partners in the Whitewater venture.[10]

In 1980, after Clinton lost his reelection bid for governor, McDougal decided to go into banking, and acquired the Bank of Kingston in 1980 and the Woodruff Savings & Loan in 1982; he then renamed the two as the Madison Bank & Trust and the Madison Guaranty Savings & Loan, respectively. In spring 1985, a fund-raiser held by McDougal Madison's office was held to pay off the remaining 1984 gubernatorial campaign debt of $50,000; McDougal raised $35,000, $12,000 of which was made up of Madison cashier's checks.[11]

That same year, McDougal decided to invest in local residential construction on a project called Castle Grande. However, the project was pricier than what McDougal could afford; to raise the $1.75 million needed, McDougal could borrow $600,000 (the most he could borrow according to law) and he tapped several others to help raise the additional funds. Among these was Seth Ward, an employee of the bank, who helped funnel the additional $1.15 million required by moving funds back and forth among several investors to avoid the threat of investigation. In 1986, federal regulators discovered that all the funds for the project had in fact come entirely from Madison Guaranty; the investigation saw the McDougal's resigning from Madison Guaranty. The Clintons lost between $37,000 and $69,000 on their Whitewater investment, a lesser amount than the McDougal's lost, for reasons unclear in the media reports. Also coming under question was the fact that Hilary Clinton's law firm—the Rose Law Firm—had been retained by McDougal to handle the bank's legal affairs.[12]

Beginning in 1992, as the Clinton presidential campaign was underway, the Federal Resolution Trust Corp., investigating causes of Madison's failure, notified the Justice Department that the Clintons were potential beneficiaries of illegal activities at Madison. By 1993, with the Clintons in the White House, the Justice Department announced it would subpoena the Clintons in order to investigate files pertaining to Whitewater. By December 1993, the White House agreed to turn over documents.[13]

In the meantime, Kagan along with other White House aides and advisors were trying to protect the president. Among Kagan's duties was to deflect a Senate subpoena for notes of meetings between the White House and private lawyers. Kagan also worked with former officials and law professors, who supported Clinton in trying to solicit supportive statements or op-ed articles. Kagan is said to have even ghostwritten or edited some of these documents. For instance, in a letter to Georgetown University law professor Paul Rothstein, Kagan included talking points summarizing the administration's position that conversations Clinton had with lawyers several years earlier were privileged and beyond the reach of a subpoena issued by the Senate Whitewater Committee. Kagan argued that "We are providing these to a number of people whom we hope will write opinion pieces supportive of that position." Kagan also sent almost identical letters to others who might be persuaded to draft op-ed pieces or write in support of the president. In another handwritten memo, Kagan said she was looking for help identifying people "who will support the general proposition . . . that conversations between a president's White House counsel and his private counsel, can in at least some circumstances, be privileged (under the attorney-client privilege)."[14]

PAULA JONES

In 1994, then-president Clinton faced another scandal, this time in the form of a sexual harassment lawsuit filed by a former Arkansas state employee, Paula Jones. In her lawsuit, Jones alleged that in 1991 then-governor Clinton propositioned her in a Little Rock hotel. Clinton argued that the lawsuit, which was partially underwritten by a conservative foundation, was a political effort to disrupt his presidency, and sought to have it dismissed or at least delayed until he left office. After losing before the federal appeals court in St. Louis, Mr. Clinton appealed to the Supreme Court.[15]

Kagan served as a link between the White House and private lawyers in crafting a legal argument in which they contended that a sitting president should not be forced to testify in a civil law suit about previous behavior prior to taking office. Kagan, in one memorandum, praised a brief arguing the case on narrow legal grounds, stating that "The brief (in my view correctly) downplays the question whether the president has constitutionally mandated immunity from civil suits involving pre-presidential conduct." Kagan went on to argue for discretion by a judge to postpone the president's testimony until after Clinton left office.[16]

However, the full extent of Kagan's involvement in the Paula Jones case remains unclear. This is due, in part, to the fact that many pieces of material pertaining to the case have not been released to the public. What is known about her role is that she monitored and commented on legal developments as the case made its way through the courts. In a 1996 memo, Kagan wrote, "Some ambiguous news on the Paula Jones front," as the case moved to the Supreme Court and the White House awaited to see if the court would hear the president's appeal. Kagan also noted that "The worst-case scenario is that the court has decided to deny" the president's petition, but had yet to issue an order "because someone is writing a dissent from the denial." She also saw "the best-case scenario is that one or more justices asked to postpone consideration" of the matter. The court did take the case and heard arguments in January 1997; unfortunately for the president, the court rejected Mr. Clinton's position.[17]

During this time, Kagan showed herself to be as ambitious and as focused on the politics of an issue as well as policy. At one point, she sought the top job in the Department of Justice's prestigious Office of Legal Counsel, which provides advice to the president on constitutional issues. After her interview with the deputy White House chief of staff, she later wrote a note reminding him that she had worked with then-Senate Judiciary Committee chairman Joe Biden on the 1993 confirmation hearings for Justice Ruth Bader Ginsburg, stating that Biden "strongly supports my selection" for the job. However, the post ended up going to someone else.[18]

DOMESTIC POLICY COUNCIL

By December 1996, Kagan gave notice to the White House that she would be leaving to return to the University of Chicago and her job as a professor of constitutional law. The movers were already scheduled and there were 120 law students in Chicago waiting and registered for her classes. She had even been given a going away party. But Bruce Reed, Clinton's new domestic policy chief, begged Kagan to stay. To sweeten the offer, Reed offered Kagan the number two spot on the Domestic Policy Council, which serves as the principal forum by the president for domestic policy matters, with the exception of economic issues. Reed also promised Kagan an equal partnership in running the DPC.

Later, a colleague at the University of Chicago commented on her choice to stay in Washington saying that "Elena thought going ahead in politics was the better path, "I think her preferred path was to stay there an extra year, get a really big administrative position, or a judgeship." Still, to many, Reed's choice seemed unconventional, and perhaps even an unwise choice. In the end, Kagan would surprise everyone, even leading Rahm Emanuel, then a Clinton senior adviser, to reportedly end numerous conversations daily with the words "Well, Elena better come up with some policy!"[19]

Kagan, by now, had earned a reputation as a savvy, sometimes sharp-tongued lawyer who handled the politics and bureaucratic infighting with little problem. At the beginning of her new post, Kagan was asked to describe her management style. She stated simply: "I want to be kept generally up to speed on everything. Thanks." Emails and memorandums that have been released to the public also show a personality that was gifted with a dry and playful sense of humor, as well as one favorite expression: "Eeks," which expressed surprise or consternation by Kagan. She also worked hard to stay in the loop managing countless issues and policy concerns on a daily basis. She repeatedly reminded her boss Bruce Reed that "you should cc me when you respond to e-mails from staff. I do feel rather a pest," she wrote. "It's just another 10 letters (or can you do it in 5?)." In another message, Kagan noted: "FYI: you're creating extra work for our staff by not hitting the reply to all button."[20]

The correspondence also demonstrates how hard Kagan worked to maintain the party line of the White House, though if need be, she did not have a problem going up against her boss or the president.[21] It was clear that Clinton valued Kagan's input; the two often debated policy matters back and forth. Kagan also held the president in high esteem. One memo to Bruce Reed titled "Elephantine," stated, "Look at today's AP story re the president's comments on hiring welfare recipients. . . . Absolutely amazing the way he remembers things." Kagan was also fiercely protective of the president, insisting that aides and staff put their best foot forward at all times, as the president insisted on careful preparation and writing. "Not to carp," she reportedly once told a colleague, "but on memos to the president, it's usually wise to spellcheck."[22] Still, Kagan was not so star-struck by the president that she did not take him to task on occasion.

One instance came in 1997, as Clinton was preparing to deliver his State of the Union address. Kagan took issue with a portion of the speech in which Clinton would recite a quote in apparent reference to himself. The offending item was from the Biblical prophet Isaiah: "Thou shalt raise up the foundations of many generations, and thou shalt be called the repairer of the breach, the restorer of paths to dwell in." The line is often referenced in discussions of repairing racial relations.[23]

In an email message to Mr. Reed, Ms. Kagan called it "the most preposterously presumptuous line I have ever seen," adding, "The President would deserve it if the press really came down on him for this." Mr. Clinton delivered the speech with the line in it, and when it was over Ms. Kagan sent a message to the chief speechwriter, Michael Waldman, calling the speech grand and telling him he should be proud. In another instance, when noting that Clinton had scribbled a note on child support enforcement in the margin of a *New York Times* article, Kagan wrote sarcastically to Reed, "Hasn't anyone told him not to believe our sound bites?"[24]

DEALING WITH THE ISSUES

Much as she did as an associate White House counsel, Kagan continued to monitor policy issues at the White House which often meant keeping track of several pressing items at once. Kagan gave careful attention to each, and when necessary could be blunt in her offering ideas on a matter. In October 1997, when consulted for her thoughts on a proposal over religious services and student loans, she pointed out that the proposal ran counter to positions President Clinton had taken. As stated in her memo, "I guess I have a reaction, which is that we're making the President look like a liar. . . . Who's been giving the legal advice? Education? Justice? Is our own counsel's office involved? (If not, it should be.)" Kagan also suggested that some support for religious activities should be protected and was needed. Her memo continued:

It seems to me that we have to give people a very strong signal that we need to find some way of including people who are doing service activities under the auspices of church programs. . . . At the very least, we should be able to include participants in programs that aren't "pervasively sectarian."[25]

Victims' rights legislation was another area that also saw Kagan treading carefully. In March 1997, she cautioned colleagues that pending victims' rights legislation could make it harder to convict Timothy J. McVeigh, who stood accused of the 1995 bombing of the Alfred P. Murrah Federal Building in Oklahoma City which killed 168 people. Kagan wrote in a memo, "The last thing we need is for McVeigh's lawyer to charge that we're helping to create a climate that will prevent McVeigh from getting a fair trial." In reference to a proposed effort to speak to child support using a gender-neutral tone in a radio address, Kagan resisted, stating "Child support is, for the most part, about helping mothers. . . . Maybe not the mothers of the families featured in Hallmark cards, but mothers nonetheless—and lots of them."[26]

In May 1999, Kagan cautioned Vice President Al Gore to hold off on endorsing a religious freedom act; Kagan's concern was that the vice president would end up with "a gay/lesbian firestorm on your hands" if he moved too quickly. Kagan, at that time, was trying to mediate a dispute between gay groups opposing a provision in the law and various religious groups who supported the act, even though Kagan privately believed that the act was a sound one. To Gore, she wrote, "We'll let you know as soon as it's safe to go back in the water."[27]

On the issue of assisted suicide and whether to make that action a federal crime, Kagan was unusually adamant, noting in a memo that she thought the proposal "a fairly terrible idea." In the area of affirmative action, Kagan endorsed a plan that would avoid a Supreme Court ruling against affirmative action. Kagan was also involved in President Clinton's initiative to improve race relations in America. In one instance, she expressed skepticism over a proposed executive order that would allow the Justice Department to coordinate civil rights enforcement across agencies and of a drive to eliminate tracking young students by ability. "I'm not keen on the paired testing proposal—it will only encourage [Newt] Gingrich (then-Republican Speaker of the House) in his opposition to this enforcement technique," Kagan wrote,

"And I have to admit that the use of ability groupings seems to me properly a local issue, but I may be wrong about this."[28]

During the course of her time in the White House, Kagan demonstrated a talent for balancing policy and politics. One example of this came with a memo about a lawsuit filed by a white teacher who, for diversity reasons, had been laid off instead of a black colleague with equal seniority. Acting solicitor general, Walter Dellinger who wrote the memo, argued that the Justice Department should file a brief backing the white teacher, but only by using very narrow reasoning in order to avoid jeopardizing affirmative action programs. Kagan agreed, writing, "I think this is exactly the right position—as a legal matter, as a policy matter, and as a political matter."[29]

When necessary, Kagan could be sharp in her notes and memos, such as a 1997 letter from a Social Security Administration official over legislation which would deny benefits to Nazi war criminals. Although Kagan took no position on the matter, she did object to the tone of the letter, stating, "This is a pretty snotty letter."[30]

Kagan did not always get along with her colleagues. Jamie Gorelick, a deputy attorney general in the Clinton administration, told the *New York Sun* in 2006 that while she admired Kagan, she also found her to be demanding and brusque. Said Gorelick: "She was extremely aggressive when she was in the White House in trying to carry out the president's agenda. . . . She was not the most popular person there in part because of that." Kagan had also earned a reputation for demanding—sometimes harshly—precision in policy statements, and it was not uncommon for her to return drafts to their authors for more revisions. "If you delivered, she liked you a lot. And if you didn't, she made sure you understood you needed to do it," recalled Chris Jennings, who directed health policy in the White House at the time. Still, for all her forthrightness, Kagan had boundaries too. When asked if a statement from the president could be altered after it had been issued, Kagan wrote, "Correcting written statements after the fact? Sounds a bit Orwellian methinks."[31]

TAKING ON TOBACCO

Certainly, one of the biggest battles faced by the Clinton administration was over tobacco. And for Kagan, the fight over tobacco proved to be the one issue where people really began paying attention to her. In creating a deal that satisfied many different parties—Congress, public health advocates, states, and tobacco companies—Kagan emerged as a political player to be reckoned with. It was her first high-profile role, and during the process she would demonstrate the traits that she has since become known for: seeking compromise in the face of a difficult situation while utilizing her command and knowledge of legal and policy issues to win over people more powerful than she.[32]

Kagan's first exposure to the tobacco fray came in 1995 when she was first hired as assistant White House counsel. At that time, the Clinton administration was in the midst of developing a strategy working with state attorneys general, trial lawyers, and public health officials about how to reduce smoking and recoup public health costs. After Kagan's promotion in 1997 as deputy domestic policy adviser, she then took the lead to implement legislation that would complete a historic $368.5 billion settlement that the tobacco companies had agreed to pay to help cover state health costs caused by smoking. The legislation was a complex issue; not only did it need to define the new authority of the Food and Drug Administration to regulate tobacco, it would also limit the tobacco industry's future liability. The latter was one condition stipulated by the tobacco companies in order for the administration to get its support. The legislation would also need to establish fees and taxes for the tobacco industry as well as place limits on tobacco advertising.[33]

Initially, many were surprised that the White House had placed such a junior person in charge of such an important task. Richard Daynard, chairman of Northeastern University's Tobacco Products Liability Project, in a later interview remembered going to the White House for a meeting. Even though the meeting was handled by then Health and Human Services secretary Donna Shalala with Kagan's boss Bruce Reed also present, Daynard's attention was drawn to a younger woman sitting behind the two. A colleague explained to Daynard that "The one who's really running this thing is neither Bruce or Donna but someone called Elena Kagan."[34]

In an ironic twist, Kagan was reminded of her own teenage smoking years; in fact, by the time she began working on the proposed legislation she had only stopped smoking for three years, having quit in 1993. In a magazine interview, she recalled, "I love smoking, and I still miss it," she says. "It's completely clear to me how addictive this product is. But it's also clear to me how much people can enjoy smoking."[35]

Kagan had her work cut out for her. Battle lines had already been drawn over the proposed settlement: state officials thought the administration was not doing enough to promote the settlement, while public health officials viewed the settlement a sellout because it included liability caps. To complicate things further, the president was facing yet another scandal when news of his dalliance with Monica Lewinsky exploded. Amid this uncertainty, Kagan presented an assertive front, taking Congress to task in order to pass this sweeping piece of legislation. Speaking in January 1998, Kagan admonished, "We shouldn't content ourselves with half measures that won't work. . . . We think people will be embarrassed to go home without doing anything."[36]

Behind the scenes, Kagan was working with a number of senators, including John McCain, the Republican senator from Arizona, and Bill Frist, the Republican senator from Tennessee, to negotiate a compromise that could get a majority of Senate votes. Unfortunately, one of the major sticking points was the provision which would allow the FDA to regulate tobacco; some senators feared that it would give the agency too much power. Kagan offered an alternative which would allow the FDA to regulate tobacco under a new, separate authority. She also crafted another compromise measure which addressed worries that the FDA would try to regulate tobacco farmers. As one person later remarked, Kagan was "pragmatic in the sense that she understood that compromise was necessary in order to achieve this huge public health objective. . . . But she was also smart enough to know that the FDA needed to get behind it and that their substantive and legal expertise couldn't be second-guessed. That was a very important balance."[37]

Meanwhile, Kagan also had to address Justice Department concerns that the proposed liability limits and advertising restrictions would pass legal muster; she managed to successfully quell those concerns. David Ogden, who was then the deputy attorney general, recalled that Kagan was "always respectful, but also quite forceful. . . . She didn't give ground that she didn't think she needed to give. She was thoughtful in listening to valid points, but if you didn't have a valid point she pushed you until it was clear that you didn't. She was very good at that."[38]

To her credit, Kagan's efforts in working with senators and agencies finally bore fruit when the Senate Commerce Committee approved the bill in April 1998 on a 19–1 vote; during the vote John McCain took to the floor to make a point of crediting Kagan for her hard work. But the legislation ran into trouble on the floor of the Senate. The White House and Congress, seeing tobacco as an easy revenue source, had added additional taxes and fees, ballooning the settlement into a $500 billion package. The industry had had enough: It launched a $50 million ad campaign, casting the bill as a giant tax increase. That June, the bill collapsed a few votes shy 60; the bill was not only dead, but so was the settlement. Five months later, the states agreed to a $206 billion settlement which lacked many of the earlier provisions that Kagan and the others had worked so hard to include.[39]

Kagan, although disappointed, still tried to force Congress into revisiting the proposed reforms of the earlier settlement package by threatening that the federal government would claim half of the states' settlement to cover its share of health costs. But her efforts came to little avail, and by the end of 1999, she was gone from the White House. At that point, Kagan admitted in a newspaper article that she was doubtful of staying for the rest of Clinton's second term. "I miss the academic life," she said, though she admitted, even though she tried to "vanquish tobacco" she would "still smoke the occasional cigar."[40]

Kagan's ambitions were still on claiming a seat on the bench. In 1999, President Clinton nominated her to a seat on the federal appeals court for the District of Columbia. It was the same court where Kagan had clerked for Abner Mikva many years ago. But politics interfered and her nomination fell through due to Republican refusal to schedule a hearing. The seat eventually went to John G. Roberts Jr., now the chief justice of the Supreme Court. Kagan was at loose ends; not wanting to stay in Washington, she now weighed her options.

NOTES

1. Amy Goldstein, Carol D. Leonnig, and Peter Slevin, "For Supreme Court Nominee Elena Kagan, a History of Pragmatism over Partisanship," *Washington Post*, May 11, 2010, http://www.washington

post.com/wp-dyn/content/article/2010/05/10/AR2010051002787
.html?sid=ST201008050526.

2. Carl Hulse, "Bill Clinton Speaks Out on Court Nominee, Recalling Her Service in the White House," *New York Times*, June 20, 2010, Section A, p. 23.

3. Peter Baker, Sheryl Gay Stolberg, Charlie Savage, and Adam Liptak, "As Counsel, Kagan Gave Advice on Volatile Issues," *New York Times*, June 12, 2010, p. 11.

4. Ibid.

5. Ibid.

6. Ibid.

7. Ibid.

8. Ibid.

9. Ibid.

10. "Whitewater Timeline," *Washington Post*, 1998, http://www
.washingtonpost.com/wp-srv/politics/special/whitewater/timeline.htm.

11. Ibid.

12. Ibid.

13. Ibid.

14. Bill Mears, "Kagan Documents Reveal Role in Whitewater Negotiations," *CNN.Politics*, June 11, 2012, http://www.cnn.com/2010/POLITICS/06/11/scotus.kagan.documents/index.html.

15. Jess Bravin, "Kagan Worked on Jones Lawsuit for Clinton," *Wall Street Journal*, June 12, 2010, http://online.wsj.com/article/SB10001424052748703509404575300382609656828.html.

16. Baker, Stolberg, Savage, and Liptak, "As Counsel, Kagan Gave Advice on Volatile Issues."

17. Bravin, "Kagan Worked on Jones Lawsuit for Clinton."

18. Baker, Stolberg, Savage, and Liptak, "As Counsel, Kagan Gave Advice on Volatile Issues."

19. Sheryl Gay Stolberg, Katherine Q. Seelye, and Lisa W. Foderaro, "Pragmatic New Yorker Chose A Careful Path to Washington," *New York Times*, May 11, 2010, Section A, p.1; Dana Milbank, "Wonderwonk," *New Republic*, May 18, 1998, http://www.newrepublic.com/article/politics/wonderwonk#; Jonathan Strong and Jon Ward, "What's in Supreme Court Nominee Elena Kagan's Clinton-Era White House Memos?" *Daily Caller*, May 11, 2010, http://dailycaller.com/2010/05/11/

what%E2%80%99s-in-supreme-court-nominee-elena-kagan%E2%80%99s-clinton-era-white-house-memos/.

20. Strong and Ward, "What's in Supreme Court Nominee Elena Kagan's Clinton-era White House memos?"

21. Associated Press, "160,000 Docs Released from Clinton Library Reveal Elena Kagan Favors Politics over Policy," *New York Daily News*, June 19, 2010, http://www.nydailynews.com/news/politics/160–000-docs-released-clinton-library-reveal-elana-kagan-favors-politics-pol icy-article-1.180715.

22. Strong and Ward, "What's in Supreme Court Nominee Elena Kagan's Clinton-Era White House Memos?"; Associated Press, "160,000 Docs Released from Clinton Library Reveal Elena Kagan Favors Politics over Policy."

23. Associated Press, "160,000 Docs Released from Clinton Library Reveal Elena Kagan Favors Politics over Policy."

24. Ibid.

25. Adam Liptak and Sheryl Gay Stolberg, "Kagan's E-Mail at Clinton White House Reveals a Blunt, Savvy Legal Adviser," *New York Times*, June 18, 2010, http://www.nytimes.com/2010/06/19/us/politics/19kagan.html?_r=0.

26. Ibid.

27. Associated Press, "160,000 Docs Released from Clinton Library Reveal Elena Kagan Favors Politics over Policy."

28. Liptak and Stolberg, "Kagan's E-Mail at Clinton White House Reveals a Blunt, Savvy Legal Adviser."

29. Ibid.

30. Sheryl Gay Stolberg, "Glimpses of Kagan's Views in White House," *New York Times*, June 4, 2012, http://www.nytimes.com/2010/06/05/us/politics/05kagan.html?_r=0.

31. Goldstein, Leonnig, and Slevin, "For Supreme Court Nominee Elena Kagan, a History of Pragmatism over Partisanship"; Liptak and Stolberg, "Kagan's E-Mail at Clinton White House Reveals a Blunt, Savvy Legal Adviser."

32. Alec MacGinnis, "Elena Kagan Has Been Battle Tested by Tobacco Legislation in the '90s," *Washington Post*, June 4, 2010, http://www.washingtonpost.com/wp-dyn/content/article/2010/06/03/AR2010060303536.html.

33. Ibid.

34. Ibid.

35. Dana Milbank, "Wonderwonk," *New Republic*, May 18, 1998, http://www.newrepublic.com/article/politics/wonderwonk#.

36. MacGinnis, "Elena Kagan Has Been Battle Tested by Tobacco Legislation in the '90s."

37. Ibid.

38. Ibid.

39. Ibid.

40. Milbank, "Wonderwonk."

41. Goldstein, Leonnig, and Slevin, "For Supreme Court Nominee Elena Kagan, a History of Pragmatism over Partisanship."

Chapter 8

HARVARD AND WASHINGTON

Elena Kagan was still considering what to do as she prepared to leave Washington. She thought she would return to Chicago; however, if she wanted to continue teaching at the University of Chicago Law School, she would have to be reappointed. By choosing to stay on at the Clinton White House, she had forfeited her academic leave.

Kagan knew that going back to Chicago was a bit of a risk. Although she had her supporters on the law school faculty, she also had more than her share of detractors as well. And to win her job back, Kagan would need to subject herself to a faculty vote—the only way she would be able to return was if the faculty allowed her to come back. As one former colleague remarked, "There's a Chicago attitude that people who [have] spent that long in Washington are not really people who will come back and roll up their sleeves and be full-time scholars." Another faculty member stated that Kagan's opponents believed that she was not "really committed to the academy and didn't really show promise as a first-rate scholar," a claim that the faculty member dismissed as "really stupid."[1]

In the end, there was no vote taken for Kagan, but then no job offer appeared either. But another school beckoned: Harvard Law School,

Kagan's alma mater. Law school friends who were teaching there recruited her to return to Harvard to teach. And, so it was in 1999 that
Elena Kagan moved again—this time to Cambridge, Massachusetts,
and Harvard Law School as an assistant professor. Who knew that little
more than a year later, she would be offered tenure, and that in four
years of her arrival on campus, Elena Kagan would rise to the office of
the dean.

PROFESSOR KAGAN

Like her time at Chicago, Kagan soon became a popular professor on
the campus. Although the job was clearly a look-see, it was clear to
many on the faculty that Kagan was popular with many students. As a
professor, she was demanding and energetic, while possessed of a self-
deprecating wit. Kagan became involved in the campus life, which
included workshops to comment on colleagues' writings, advising the
law review board, as well as having dinner with faculty members.[2]

Not everyone was enamored of Kagan or her teaching style. As one
former student wrote years later:

> Kagan was a frightening professor for those who wanted to match
> wits with the brightest legal minds in the world. For people like
> me, people who just wanted to get through law school with mini-
> mal mental damage, Kagan was nothing short of terrifying. . . .
> As a professor, Kagan was one of the last of a dying breed: a
> purely Socratic law school professor. With Kagan, there was no
> panel. There was no back-benching. She would just randomly
> call . . . and you had best be prepared.[3]

The student also went on to recount that Kagan could not abide
tardiness in her students and would literally stop class, even to the
point where she would stop speaking until the student had taken a
seat. Kagan also could not abide students who were unprepared for
class:

Professor Kagan:	Well, Mr. Mystal, did you manage to remem-ber your casebook?
11 Elie:	Yes. But like I said, I didn't . . .

Professor Kagan:	Do you think you could be bothered to OPEN your casebook?
1l Elie:	(I have a bad feeling about this.) Yes. Abso . . .
Professor Kagan:	Please turn to page [whatever]. . . . Now read.
1l Elie:	(Reading silently.)
Professor Kagan:	ALOUD.
1l Elie:	. . . Umm . . . Okay. (Much reading aloud.)
Professor Kagan:	Now, can you explain to me what you just read?
1l Elie:	(I can't even remember what I blathered.)
Professor Kagan:	Mr. Mystal, open to page [same page as before], and TRY AGAIN![4]

SEEKING SOLUTIONS

During Kagan's time as professor, the campus was involved in the contentious issue of expansion. For some time, Harvard had been buying up properties beyond Cambridge, specifically in the Boston neighborhood of Allston, located across the Charles River from the university. It was initially hoped that the law school would eventually move to the neighborhood; however, the law faculty voted a resounding no to the proposition with the final vote of 37–1. As one professor later commented on the rare show of solidarity by the faculty, "It's rare that anyone here agrees about anything, but everyone agreed we didn't want our campus moved across the river."[5]

With the installation of Lawrence H. Summers as the new president of Harvard in 2001, the issue of the Allston neighborhood was back on the table. By that time, the dean of the Law School, Robert C. Clark, asked Kagan, now newly tenured, to head up a study committee; Clark also had another reason for choosing Kagan. He saw her as a potential successor to his position as dean and wanted to see how she would handle a leadership role and a controversial issue. Clark was not disappointed. "Her approach was to give a rational basis, instead of just an emotional one, for the faculty's reaction," in explaining their position to President Summers, Clark later stated.[6]

Among the actions Kagan took included s the hiring of a consultant whom she convinced the university to pay for. The outcome of that hiring was the creation of a strategic plan that considered many different factors as to why the Law School needed to stay in Cambridge. The study concluded that although Allston was certainly ripe for the expansion of the university, it would be better suited for the biomedical schools rather than the Law School. At that point, any idea of moving the Law School was shelved. The plan was soon dead, and Kagan emerged as a folk hero on campus. As one faculty member described it, "I didn't think we had a snowball's chance," while another admitted that Kagan's "stock went way up on the reputational grapevine on the strength of that report."[7]

In November 2002, Dean Clark announced he would be stepping down as dean of the Law School. President Summers then appointed a search committee to look for a new replacement. Even though Kagan's name was mentioned, the Harvard president was not entirely sure about having Kagan aboard. One person familiar with the search process later stated in an interview that Summers had reservations about appointing Kagan to the position as "He wasn't entirely sure he could trust her to make the right kind of scholarly judgments."

Summers's reservations were also thought to be tied in to the fact that Kagan refused to become embroiled in an earlier controversy over the president's impolitic remarks about women's lack of aptitude for the sciences, remarks that in the end cost Summers his job. Even as friends of Summers asked Kagan to publicly defend him, she refused (even though, privately, Kagan believed that the flap over the president's remarks were overblown). Summers was said to have viewed Kagan's refusal as an act of disloyalty. As one faculty member described it, "She [Kagan] doesn't avoid getting engaged in issues that are controversial," he said. "But she doesn't herself want to be the object of controversy."[8]

In the meantime, other candidates were interviewed for the position of dean, while Kagan flew to the University of Texas at Austin to interview for a dean's position at that school. When asked by Harvard law professors about the position at Harvard, Kagan stated that she was not interested. As one colleague recalled, Kagan never even gave a hint that she was under consideration or that she would even take the position if offered. In the end though, Kagan emerged as the best choice; for Summers, her ability to work with others was a deciding factor. As Summers later stated, "I would say Elena's colleagues chose

Lawrence Summers (left), president of Harvard University, and a member of his staff congratulating Elena Kagan as the first woman dean of Harvard Law School in 2003. (AP Photo/Elise Amendola)

her as much as I did," though he did tell her, "Elena, if you accept this job and then you are offered a position like Supreme Court justice or attorney general, I will congratulate you with all my heart and wish you well. But we need you to make a commitment to the law school for a few years before taking any other position," a stipulation to which Kagan agreed to honor.[9]

MAINTAINING A BALANCE

The law school campus that Kagan inherited as dean was a campus divided among factional and ideological lines, particularly among the faculty. One of the first things that Kagan did was to try and mediate between the liberal and conservative factions among professors and the students. She recruited prominent conservatives and liberal candidates to join the faculty; Kagan also invited prominent conservatives to come speak. As one faculty member later recounted, Kagan was "just incredibly politically skillful" not only at recruiting, but also selling new faculty members to the existing Harvard Law School faculty. Some of the most left-leaning members of the faculty, however, stopped going to faculty meetings because they believed that important discussions were "truncated and disagreements simply glossed over." Said one anonymous critic, "I think she has a political heart. She wants to do good, but she has no soul, no center of gravity, so her heart can move depending on the political moment."[10]

During her time as dean, Kagan hired 43 faculty members, increasing the number of full-time law school faculty from 81 to 104 members. Even though Kagan was accused later of not making enough minority hires, overall the faculty was more content than it had been in a long time. It also helped that Harvard was enjoying an abundant endowment during this period, as well as a successful and a record-setting $476.5 million fund-raising drive that was begun under the previous dean and which Kagan saw through to its conclusion. To help professors to get to know each other, Kagan arranged a faculty lounge which offered free lunches where faculty members could gather and eat at large tables. The atmosphere promoted a sense if not of camaraderie, but certainly community, leading one faculty member to pronounce the effort an "absolute stroke of genius."[11]

Noo matter the situation, Kagan did not wait to see what others thought of her ideas—she often moved forward with plans despite faculty grumblings. As one faculty member stated, Kagan "has superb interpersonal skills, but she is not someone who has a compelling need to have everyone like her and to have everyone approve of what ultimately she is trying to achieve." Still, other faculty members did not see Kagan's "interpersonal skills" in the same way. On the occasion of hiring conservative thinker and former George W. Bush cabinet member Jack Goldsmith, one faculty member who had misgivings about the hire stated, "We had differing views," and that he believed Kagan to be "rather dismissive" of his opinion.[12]

Still many faculty members found Kagan to be a "strategic and deliberative thinker on all issues," who always had a sense of "Let me do my homework" in order to prepare for discussions. Kagan's dedication to the job was unquestioned; she met with every member of the faculty, and as one professor noted, "She was willing to work seven days a week, it wasn't just Monday through Friday, 10 to 5, it was whenever people were available—a baseball game, a student reception, a breakfast, a lunch, a coffee."[13]

But even with Kagan's successes, many realized that her energies were spent not so much in consensus building, but in the more skillful navigation of the tricky waters that marked Harvard faculty politics as well giving grease to accelerate the process, of building key relationships not just within the law faculty, but with other departments on the campus too. Kagan's successes also came from her ability to build relationships on both sides of the political fence as well as having no qualms to ram proposals through. As one conservative onlooker commented, "She knocked some heads. . . . And she made people realize it couldn't go on because we were aging, and we weren't replacing ourselves, and we needed to grow." A more liberal faculty member agreed with this assessment saying, "My own judgment is that running the place with a fairly heavy hand . . . was politically necessary in order to get the faculty to move forward."[14]

Still, many on campus believe Kagan was a "gracious and generous" dean, who was fond of celebrating people's accomplishments whether putting a new book on display or featuring a panel. Many now viewed the law school in a new light, as a place that was much more "intellectually vibrant," as well as a happier place. Even though Kagan was characterized as a "master pool shark, and we are all the balls she is shooting in the pockets," said one supporter, the fact was Kagan got things done.[15]

IMPROVING STUDENT LIFE

In addition to working on improving faculty relations at the law school, Kagan took the initiative to improve student life on the campus. According to one faculty member, "Harvard was not a warm and fuzzy place. It was a tough experience for many, and in a variety of ways large and small she focused energy on the question how can we improve the student experience." This included implementing upgrades to the physical campus, such as a refurbished student center and gym. Kagan had an area outside turned into an ice-skating rink for the students during the winter, which doubled as a volleyball court in warmer weather. Free coffee was available for students outside classrooms and the women's restrooms now had free tampons. Students were also consulted about the placement of art in what were otherwise cold and barren hallways. Kagan also worked tirelessly to promote public service careers for graduating law students, as well as overhauling an outdated first-year curriculum and reducing class sizes.[16]

One student remembered how Kagan would try to be accessible to the students; it was not uncommon in good weather to see the dean outside reading on a bench near her office. She was happy to talk to students and many surprisingly found that when they emailed Kagan, they generally had a response within the hour. She arrived at work dressed in a suit with sneakers. She still smoked on occasion and more than one student would see her coming out of a store with a bottle of wine. She still maintained her reputation as a cut-throat poker player. Kagan knew what Harvard Law School represented to many of its students and she encouraged students to have fun as well as hitting the books. "She appreciated that law school was an opportunity not only to learn the law but also to learn how to ice skate," one student later remarked.[17]

THE FEDERALIST SOCIETY

In an attempt to add more balance to the liberal-slanted campus life, Kagan worked particularly hard to reach out to student conservatives. Her efforts in large part, were a success. For example, members of the national conservative group the Federalist Society, who had a chapter on campus, had shirts printed with Kagan's likeness and the statement, "I love the Federalist Society!," a reference to a remark Kagan made at the national convention of the conservative Federalist Society that met at the campus. As Kagan later told the story to a reporter, "I looked out at them and said, 'You are not my people,' and everyone laughed, and then I said, 'But I love the Federalist Society,' and I think that is when I got a standing ovation. People, it turns out, loved to be told that they are loved." As one member of the organization later said, "She was a very effective dean . . . Kagan treated the conservative student organizations not like they were some kind of pesky fly but rather serious organizations."[18]

DON'T ASK, DON'T TELL

Around Christmas 2004, Dean Kagan made a phone call to the home of a third year law student, who was the leader of a small club composed of military veterans. She requested that the student come to her office, as she had something she wished to speak to him about. When the student arrived, Kagan began talking about the matter of military recruiting on campus and made a surprising request. Because the law school had recently stopped sponsoring recruiters from the armed services, Kagan asked that the veterans club instead take on the task of recruiting interviews. In the end, the veteran's group turned down the request because as one student veteran explained, "we are basically students, not recruiters."[19]

Few realized at the time that Kagan was actually pursuing two courses of action with regard to the military on the Harvard Law School campus. One, she was taking a tough stance on having recruiters on campus because of the military's ban on homosexual men and women serving in the armed services openly and two, she was still trying to accommodate some type of recruiting activity on campus. For Kagan watchers, it was typical Kagan maneuvering, as many thought she was hedging on making tough decisions as well as simply trying to stay afloat in the murky waters of Harvard campus politics and not antagonize rival campus groups.

Although Kagan would later be accused of having hostile feelings toward the military, veterans attending the law school at Harvard have stated that those opinions are not accurate. The truth was, recruiters, though not officially sponsored on campus in the spring of 2005, were able to carry on recruiting activities without interference from Kagan. If anything, the episode illustrated how successfully Kagan separated her private feelings over the matter from public policy on the campus.[20]

Kagan had inherited the recruiting controversy when she became dean in 2003. It was a widespread issue that was debated in many law schools throughout the nation. At the crux of the controversy was the military's "don't ask, don't tell" rule (in which homosexual members of the armed forces could not openly admit their homosexuality) as violating campus antidiscrimination policies. But the problem was not a simple one. In order to receive federal aid, schools needed to sponsor recruiters. Harvard was sponsoring recruiters by the time Kagan became dean, even though personally Kagan was an outspoken opponent to the "don't ask, don't tell" policy. A year later, Harvard, along with a group of other law schools, would file suit with the U.S. Court of Appeals for the Third Circuit arguing that the law, known as the Solomon Amendment, which linked federal aid to recruiting help was unconstitutional.

In filing a "friend of the court" brief opposing the amendment, Kagan and others argued that the military's ban on gays violated the law school's right to prohibit employers who discriminate on the basis of sexual orientation. In the brief, Kagan called the ban "a moral injustice of the first order," adding, "The importance of the military to our society—and the extraordinary service that members of the military provide to all the rest of us—makes this discrimination more, not less, repugnant." On the heels of the lawsuit, Kagan announced that Harvard would no longer provide such help to military recruiters, becoming the only school to do so.[21]

By the fall of 2004, Kagan realized that the court would soon hand down a decision; it was then that she offered to meet with the veterans group on campus in order to discuss the issue. One alumnus of the school and the organization at that time asked the dean whether the law linking federal aid to military recruiting might have an analogy: the Federal Highway Administration did not give states money if their legal drinking age was lower than 21; the response was laughter on the part of the students. But Kagan was not amused, telling the group that as dean she felt "mocked." According to one witness, "The room dropped several degrees, and we had to sort of defuse the situation," and assure Kagan that the group was not making fun of her.[22]

Not long after the Third Circuit ruling, which struck down the amendment lawsuit brought by the schools, Kagan directed the school's Office of Career Services to stop providing help to military recruiters, although in a letter to the law school faculty, she stated that the military retained full access to students through the Harvard Law School Veterans Association. It was then that the head of the campus veterans group heard from Kagan, requesting that he come to her office where she made her request for the group to take on recruiting activities for the campus. The meeting lasted only 20 minutes with the student stating that he had to consult with the other members before a decision could be made. The group debated long and hard over what to do; some supported helping the recruiters, saying that the military needed well-trained lawyers during wartime. One student stated that he believed that Kagan should not oppose military recruiting and the ban on gays, then try to come up with another solution to let recruiters in. He later stated, "I didn't want to make my first act at law school ushering in the military through the back door. . . . If you are going to take a stand against it, take a stand against it. . . . Don't play games." Finally, the group agreed to allow the association handle questions from students interested in military careers, but that the group would do nothing more. "We took the request in good faith and, at the end of the day, thought, 'Hey, the military has its own recruiters,'" the former leader said.[23]

In the end, Kagan's decision had no impact on the number of people entering the military from Harvard; that spring, 2005, five graduates joined up, more than any other year of that decade. A colleague of Kagan's later remarked that the incident "was very difficult for Elena. . . . This was a decision you can't win. You are either going to alienate the gay students and everyone who was sympathetic to their cause, or the veterans and those students who are sympathetic to their cause." The colleague also recalled Kagan stating, "I want to do stuff to make the students feel that Harvard supports them, supports their service to the country."[24]

During the fall of 2006, Kagan did two things. She first inaugurated an intimate dinner with the veterans attending law school; it was to become an annual tradition held every Veterans Day until she left Harvard in 2007. Also during that fall, a veteran was a finalist in Harvard's Ames Moot Court competition where Supreme Court Justice Anthony M. Kennedy was a judge. At a dinner before the arguments, Kennedy spoke with a student, who was preparing to be a military lawyer; he told the student stories about his own time in the California National Guard. As they took their seats, Kennedy leaned over to Kagan, saying he hoped that she took the time to recognize the veterans attending the law school. Kagan assured Kennedy she did.[25]

Robert Merrill, a former Marine who attended Harvard during Kagan's tenure as dean, believes that Kagan was never antimilitary during the Solomon Amendment controversy. In an article published in 2010, Merrill stated:

> If anything, Kagan was an activist in ensuring that military recruiters had viable access to students and facilities despite the official ban. A Boston-area recruiter later told me that the biggest hurdle he faced recruiting at Harvard Law was trying to answer the students' strangely intellectual questions. Kagan's Veterans Day dinners became a tradition. During my final year at Harvard, she treated the veterans to dinner at a restaurant in Cambridge. (Military service has its perks.) Again, there was no agenda other than to thank us for our service and to ask about our military experiences. Over wine and dinner, Kagan listened attentively to our war stories. I later told her that her blunt style of leadership would have served her well in the Marines.[26]

AMBITION

By 2007, Lawrence Summers was gone as the president of Harvard. Several hoped that Kagan would now be tapped to head the university as its president. Though Kagan herself wanted the job, she was cautious to not openly campaign for the position. Still many on the campus believed that Kagan was a shoo-in for the job. Her many successes at the Law School seemed to ensure the presidency for her. One student later said that "We all thought she would get it, and we were scared that she would leave and that all the changes she had implemented would no longer be kept up."[27]

But there were rumblings among the members of the search committee that Kagan was not all she appeared to be. Reports of her behavior with her staff as being too harsh did not sit well. Criticism of Kagan's thin scholarly input was raised. Then, there was the history of the school itself; only one previous dean of the law school had ascended the president's chair in the school's entire history; other presidents had been picked from the fields of science or the humanities. In the end, historian Drew Gilpin Faust was chosen for the position.[28]

Law students, however, gave Kagan a party with hundreds of them showing up wearing "I ♥ EK" T-shirts; Kagan teared up at the sight and told the students, "Sometimes, you win by losing. . . . All of you have made me feel like a real winner today." At the same time that Kagan was considering whether or not to continue at Harvard, a colleague reminded her that there was a good possibility that change would come again to Washington, D.C. A Democratic senator from Illinois named Barack Obama had recently announced his intention to run for the office of the presidency. If a Democrat won in 2008, there might be a place for Kagan in the new administration. He later recalled that Kagan "was disappointed not to be selected, as anyone would be. . . . I remember saying to her, 'I can understand why you would want this, but what if a Democrat wins the White House? You could be on the Supreme Court.' She nodded, but it wasn't like she said, 'Yeah, I'm really glad I didn't get that.'"[29]

As it turned out, Washington would, in fact, be a big part of Kagan's future soon.

NOTES

1. Amy Goldstein, Carol D. Leonnig, and Peter Slevin, "For Supreme Court Nominee Elena Kagan, a History of Pragmatism over Partisanship," *Washington Post*, May 11, 2010, http://www.washingtonpost.com/wp-dyn/content/article/2010/05/10/AR2010051002787.html?sid=ST2010080505264.

2. Sheryl Gay Stolberg, "At Harvard, Kagan Aimed Sights Higher," *New York Times*, May 25, 2010, http://www.nytimes.com/2010/05/26/us/politics/26kagan.html?pagewanted=all&_r=0.

3. Elie Mystal, "Elena Kagan and Me: One Semester of Civ Pro with the New SCOTUS Nominee," *Above the Law*, n.d., http://abovethelaw.com/2010/05/elena-kagan-and-me-one-semester-of-civ-pro-with-the-new-scotus-nominee/.

4. Ibid.

5. Stolberg, "At Harvard, Kagan Aimed Sights Higher."

6. Ibid.

7. Ibid.

8. Ibid.

9. Ibid.

10. Nina Totenberg, "At Harvard, Kagan Won More Fans than Foes," *NPR*, May 18, 2010, http://www.npr.org/templates/story/story.php?story Id=126826571.

11. Laura Meckler, "Grading Kagan as Dean: Kagan Built Bridges on Divided Campus, but Other Factors Helped Her Along," *Wall Street Journal*, May 12, 2010, http://online.wsj.com/article/SB10001424052 74870356580457523874086226702.html.

12. Ibid.

13. Stolberg, "At Harvard, Kagan Aimed Sights Higher."

14. Totenberg, "At Harvard, Kagan Won More Fans than Foes."

15. Ibid.

16. Meckler, "Grading Kagan as Dean"; Goldstein, Leonnig, and Slevin, "For Supreme Court Nominee Elena Kagan, a History of Pragmatism over Partisanship."

17. Meckler, "Grading Kagan as Dean."

18. Goldstein, Leonnig, and Slevin, "For Supreme Court Nominee Elena Kagan, a History of Pragmatism over Partisanship."

19. Amy Goldstein, "Kagan, as Harvard Law School Dean, Pursued Two Courses on 'Don't Ask' Policy," *Washington Post*, May 28, 2010, http://www.washingtonpost.com/wp-dyn/content/article/2010/05/27/AR2010052705686.html.

20. Ibid.

21. Ibid.; Robert Barnes, "High Court Nominee Never Let Lack Of Experience Hold Her Back," *Washington Post*, May 10, 2010, p. A05.

22. Goldstein, "Kagan, as Harvard Law School Dean, Pursued Two Courses on 'Don't Ask' Policy."

23. Ibid.; Barnes, "High court Nominee Never Let Lack Of Experience Hold Her Back."

24. Goldstein, "Kagan, as Harvard Law School Dean, Pursued Two Courses on 'Don't Ask' Policy."

25. Ibid.

26. Robert Merrill, "A veteran's Harvard Ally: Elena Kagan," *Washington Post*, May 21, 2010, http://www.washingtonpost.com/wp-dyn/content/article/2010/05/20/AR2010052003940.html.

27. Stolberg, "At Harvard, Kagan Aimed Sights Higher."

28. Ibid.

29. Ibid.

Chapter 9

SOLICITOR GENERAL

In January of 2009, the nation saw a number of historic firsts. With the election of Barack Obama in 2008, the United States had elected its first African American president. Not long after, Obama would set another historic precedent with the appointment of Elena Kagan as the first woman to the post of Solicitor General of the United States. The two had clearly traveled far since their days as colleagues at the University of Chicago Law School. For Kagan, her return to Washington was particularly sweet as she prepared to take on the duties of the nation's top lawyer.

SOLICITOR GENERAL

The duties of the solicitor general include the supervision and conducting of government litigation in the U.S. Supreme Court. In essence, the solicitor general serves as the attorney for the U.S. government. Approximately, two-thirds of all the cases heard before the U.S. Supreme Court involve the federal government. Now, as the chief advocate for the United States in the Supreme Court, Kagan's responsibilities would entail defending Congressional statutes, government agency regulations—when necessary—the actions of the president.

Kagan would also make the final decisions on what cases to appeal in the lower courts, a task that would often result in fielding irate phone calls every day from the agency and government heads whose cases she had decided not to appeal. Upon taking office, Kagan pledged to defend any statute or government action "as long as there is a colorable argument to be made," which meant as long as there was a reasonable case to be made, even though Kagan might not agree personally with the policy or law she was obligated to defend.[1]

THE ROAD TO CONFIRMATION

However, the road to being appointed to the post was rocky for the former Harvard Law School dean. Although widely admired for her intellectual capabilities as well as her gift for consensus building and politicking, Kagan's nomination to the office of solicitor general had one gaping void on her resume: she had never argued a case in the Supreme Court. In fact, Kagan had never argued a case in front of any court.[2]

Kagan's confirmation hearings began on February 10, 2009; for the most part, the hearings were relatively low-key and not particularly controversial. For the senators grilling Kagan, questions tended to focus on two primary issues: first, would Kagan defend statutes to which she was personally opposed, and second, was Kagan qualified to hold the position of solicitor general given her lack of courtroom experience?[3]

In addressing the first concern, Kagan repeatedly stated that whatever she might feel personally about an issue she was charged with defending, she would never let that interfere with her duties as solicitor general. As she told the committee: "When one assumes the Solicitor General's role, one is assuming a set of responsibilities—a set of obligations—of which the defense of statutes is one of the most critically important. And you defend those statutes whether you would have voted for those statutes or not." For instance, in the case of the Solomon Amendment, even though she personally found the policy of "Don't' Ask, Don't Tell" abhorrent, she would have defended the amendment because there was a "reasonable basis" for it. Conversely, Kagan was questioned on whether she would defend a statute even if the president was against it. Kagan replied that regardless of the president's stand on an issue, if she was charged with defending it, she would, stating that "presidential opposition would seldom undermine the legal basis for a statute." Kagan also discussed the one exception to that which would be in the instance of a statute infringing on a core power of the president. To make her point, Kagan referred the committee to the court case *Youngstown Sheet & Tube v. Sawyer*, a 1952 Supreme Court case in which the court severely limited the powers of the executive office in the absences of specifically stated authority under Article Two of the Constitution or statutory authority conferred on the president by the Congress. In the opinion, executive power of the president is deemed at its lowest ebb when Congress has spoken against it.[4]

Turning to national security matters, a member of the committee, Senator Lindsay Graham, stated that under military law a member of an enemy force can be detained without trial. When he queried as to how Kagan stood on the issue, she stated that "that makes sense, and I think you're correct that that is the law." She was not as forthcoming in some of her written responses, however; when asked by Senator Specter her opinion on the rights detainees held at the Bagram Air Force Base, Kagan demurred from answering, stating that she might one day have to participate in ongoing litigation on that matter.[5]

Kagan also had an opportunity to address the Solomon Amendment and her stand on it as dean of the Harvard Law School:

As the dean of a law school with a general nondiscrimination policy "meant to protect each of our students regardless of such factors as race, religion, sex, or sexual orientation" I thought the right thing to do was to defend that policy and to do so vigorously. For that reason, when the Third Circuit held the Solomon Amendment unconstitutional, I reinstated the school's policy pending the Supreme Court's decision in *Rumsfeld v. FAIR*. . . . As Solicitor General, I would have a wholly different role and set of responsibilities.[6]

In addressing the confirmation committee's second concern over Kagan's lack of legal experience, Kagan pointed out to the committee what she believed to be her qualifications for the position, including "judgment as opposed just to book learning" and her "lifetime of learning and study of the law, and particularly of the constitutional and administrative law issues that form the core of the Court's docket." She also told the skeptical members of the committee that she was not overly concerned about her perceived lack of experience in that she would be bringing into the job "a lifetime of learning and study in the law"—not just as a professor of law, but also as a lawyer both with private practice and public service, a referral to her time working in the Clinton administration. Still, not everybody on the committee was convinced; when Senators Tom Coburn and John Kyl both said they "wouldn't want a surgeon working on them with so little practical experience," Kagan, quipped "frankly anybody has some gaps."[7]

FACING THE PAST

During the hearing, Kagan was also questioned about some her opinions expressed early on in her legal career. In regard to a memorandum that she wrote as a law clerk to Justice Thurgood Marshall, Kagan first stated that it was "the dumbest thing I ever read." Then, she went on to explain:

> Let me step back a little if I may and talk about my role in Justice Marshall's chambers. . . . We wrote memos on literally every single case in which there was a petition . . . I don't want to say there is nothing of me in these memos, but I think in large measure these memos were written in the context of—you're an assistant for a justice, you're trying to facilitate his work, and to enable him to advance his goals and purposes as a justice. . . . I was a 27-year-old pipsqueak and I was working for an 80-year-old giant in the law and a person who—let us be frank—had very strong jurisprudential and legal views . . . and he was asking us in the context of those cert. petitions to channel him, and to think about what cases he would want the Court to decide. . . .

> With reference about how Supreme Court nominees should answer questions, based on her controversial book review written

in 1995, Kagan told the committee that "I'm not sure that, sitting here today, I would agree" with the position she had taken earlierIn the end, Kagan was confirmed by a vote of 61 to 31 on March 9, 2009.[8]

SOLICITOR GENERAL KAGAN

Certainly, one of the great challenges facing Kagan as solicitor general was the prospect of arguing cases in front of a Supreme Court that had grown increasingly more conservative over the years. In addition, as the first woman solicitor general, Kagan was the subject of much speculation; however, the interest was not so much about the cases Kagan would argue, but rather about what she would wear. Traditionally, all solicitors general wear a long morning coat with tails. After polling the justices to see if they would object if she chose not to wear the attire, Kagan instead opted for dark suits.[9]

When faced with the first case to be argued, Kagan passed. The case was an important voting rights case and Kagan decided to defer to the

Retired Supreme Court Justice Sandra Day O'Connor, left, speaking with U.S. Solicitor General Elena Kagan in Washington, D.C., in 2010. (AP Photo/Jose Luis Magana)

lawyers who had prepared the case. It would not be until September 2009 before Kagan would step in front of the Supreme Court for the first time as the new Solicitor General of the United States. Her first case then would be a campaign finance case known as the *Citizens United*. Despite her insistence that she was not worried about the upcoming case (she even went to the movies the night before her appearance), privately, Kagan was nervous. She would later admit that she was "nervous because it was my first one. . . . But honestly no more nervous than I've been lots of other times in my life when I've done things for the first time." She also recalled that once she spoke the first sentence, the whole experience became fun challenging [and] exciting."[10]

In a later interview, Kagan was more forthcoming about her experience:

G: Was your very first oral argument in the U.S. Supreme Court?

K: My very first appellate argument was in the U.S. Supreme Court.

G: Wow! That's incredible!

K: It was even worse than that, really: It was in the U.S. Supreme Court and it was the Citizens United case.

G: That was your first oral argument?

K: It was my first oral argument. It was an important argument. For those who don't know, it was a case that had been argued the prior term. The court had decided to reargue it and had set a couple of questions for reargument on whether the court should reverse its precedents in a couple of important cases. It was pretty clear to people that the court was ready to do something significant—to reverse those cases. So it was nerve-wracking to do an argument of that importance for my first one. But every time I got too nervous about it, I would say it's OK because we know which way this is going to come out. You're going to lose. . . .

G: I'll bet! Who was the most active questioner?

K: Gosh, I got it from all over. As you know, when you come to the court these days, you do get it from all over. But I would say Justice Scalia was a very active questioner. If I recall it right, I opened my mouth and maybe I got a sentence and a half out. And then Justice Scalia said something like "No, no, no!"—which if you know Justice Scalia, probably doesn't strike you as completely out of character for him. But I loved being questioned by Justice Scalia because you always knew where he was coming from, and he always told you what he thought was the matter with your position. But he also gave you an opportunity to answer him, so he never tried to monopolize the floor. Certainly the chief justice was a very active questioner, and I remember some questions from Justice Kennedy and from Justice Stevens. Those are the ones I recall the best.[11]

CITIZENS UNITED

Her very first case for the court was *Citizens United v. Federal Election Commission*, a case that would test Kagan's knowledge of constitutional law. In the *Citizens United* case, Kagan was asking the Supreme Court to uphold an earlier 1990 precedent which stated that the government could restrict corporations from using their general treasuries to campaign for or against political candidates running for office. But instead of relying on the logic behind the decision, Kagan instead decided to try another course of action using different arguments. Kagan knew from the beginning that the court would likely not agree with her argument, and privately was grim about the most likely outcome. However, whatever she may have felt in private was kept private as she prepared for her case.

Even though it was her first time in front of the Supreme Court, Kagan's demeanor was markedly confident; dressed in her dark suit, she maintained an almost conversational tone with the justices. The situation was not without humor too; as Kagan cranked down the lectern to meet her five foot three inch height, she remarked to the court, "This may take awhile." She was also not afraid to verbally spar with the justices, and at times seemed to relish taking the court on. At one point, Kagan bluntly pointed out that for over the past century the court had never before questioned the ban on corporate spending for candidate elections. She seemed unafraid of Justice Antonin Scalia, who later said that Kagan simply "stepped into the fire."[12]

Kagan made an early impression on Scalia; a mere 20 seconds into her first argument, Scalia stopped her midsentence with "Wait, wait, wait, wait." At another point, Scalia stopped Kagan telling her, "I don't understand what you're saying." At one point during the discussion, Scalia told Kagan that the court may have never questioned the ban on campaign financing, but then it never approved it either. Further, Congress was too self-interested to be trusted on the matter of campaign financial reform, stating, "I doubt that one can expect a body of incumbents to draw election restrictions that do not favor incumbents." Kagan simply replied that Scalia and the court were wrong.[13]

Further, Kagan pointed out both corporations and unions give money to political incumbents, so limiting the money as Congress did with the campaign finance law may have been "the single most self-denying thing that Congress has ever done." Perhaps, of all the justices, Scalia was the most invigorated by Kagan's approach and appreciated her pushing back; as he stated later in an interview: "That's what's supposed to happen. . . . The reason you ask the question is to see if there's a decent answer to it." Instead of agreeing, Chief Justice Roberts used Kagan's arguments against her, and in the end, the government lost the case. One legal expert later remarked that Kagan's decision to go another route in presenting the argument, in effect, allowed the court to rule against her. Still, the same expert also stated that given the case, it would have been difficult to win, no matter who the solicitor general was.[14]

OTHER APPEARANCES

During her 15 months as solicitor general, Kagan personally argued five other cases. Among the more notable included the 2010 case *Salazar v. Buono*, in which one of the central issues was a cross standing on government land. In 1934, the Veterans of Foreign Wars built a wooden cross on top of Sunrise Rock in the Mojave National Preserve to commemorate those who died in the First World War. Over the years, the cross was rebuilt several times. In 1999, a former Preserve employee filed suit in a California federal district court seeking to prevent the permanent display of the cross. His suit was based on the fact that when a request was made of the Preserve to construct a Buddhist shrine in the Preserve, near the cross, the request was denied. Further, the lawsuit argued that the cross's display on federal property violated the Establishment Clause of the First Amendment. The district court agreed and the cross was covered up.[15]

While the case was pending, Congress designated Sunrise Rock a national memorial and barred its dismantling with the use of federal funds. One year later, Sunrise Rock became private property as the result of a land exchange. The former employee then moved to not only enforce the previous court order preventing the display of the cross, but also to prohibit the land swap. The district court granted both motions. The Secretary of the Interior appealed, arguing that the district court abused its discretion. On appeal, the U.S. Court of Appeals for the Ninth Circuit disagreed with the Secretary stating that the government failed to show that the district court's fact findings or legal standards were clearly erroneous, nor did it show that the district court made an error in judgment.[16]

There were two issues at stake in this argument: one, could the employee, Mr. Buono, maintain his lawsuit when he is "merely offended by the fact that public land on which a cross is displayed is not a forum for other religious symbols"? The second issue was whether or not the U.S. Court of Appeals for the Ninth Circuit erred in not giving more attention to the land exchange by Congress. In her opening statement, Kagan stated that "The district court gave Congress two basic options when it found the Sunrise Rock War Memorial unconstitutional. First, Congress could accede to permanently removing the memorial, ending the dispute, but also doing away with a memorial that for 75 years had commemorated America's fallen soldiers and had acquired deep meaning for the veterans in the community." Further, with the issue of the land transfer, Kagan stated that "The government has argued—argued below that there was no violation prior to the transfer statute, and that remains the government's position . . . we think that that position has been overtaken by events and that the only question before the Court is the transfer statute." In addition, there were several pockets of privately held land among the Preserve holdings. Kagan also suggested that since the memorial belonged to the VFW, the signage or some other means of identifying the memorial would clearly define that the VFW owned the cross, not the government. In the end, the court agreed and reversed the Ninth Circuit's decision.[17]

In the 2010 case of *United States v. Comstock*, which focused on the constitutionality of a statute authorizing the civil confinement of sexually dangerous prisoners, the government argued that it was necessary to keep convicted sex offenders from endangering the lives of others. The suit was brought by a group of prisoners who moved to dismiss petitions by the government requesting their indefinite civil commitment under the Adam Walsh Child Protection and Safety Act. A North Carolina federal district court dismissed the petitions.

On appeal, the U.S. Court of Appeals for the Fourth Circuit affirmed the decision of the North Carolina court, stating that the Protection and Safety Act exceeded the authority of Congress when it enacted the Adam Walsh Child Protection and Safety Act solely because of "sexual dangerousness." Further, the government need not even allege that this "dangerousness" violated any federal law which treaded into the territory of civil rights violations. By the time the suit reached the Supreme Court, the question was did Congress have the authority to enact the Adam Walsh Protection and Safety Act?[18]

In presenting her argument for the government, Kagan stated that the practice of indefinite incarceration was necessary to "run a criminal justice system that does not itself endanger the public." Kagan relied on a clause of the Constitution that was not ordinarily considered a source of freestanding authority, that is, the clause stating that Congress has the right to "make all laws which shall be necessary and proper for carrying into execution" its other powers. Justice Scalia went after Kagan disputing her argument stating, "Necessary and proper doesn't mean it is necessary and proper for the good of society. . . . It means it is necessary and proper for the execution of another power that the federal government is given by the constitution." Scalia also offered the suggestion that state officials could handle the task without the help of the federal government.[19]

Kagan agreed with Scalia that it was up to the states to take the lead role; however, she saw the role of the federal government as a kind of "backstop, so that if the state does not take responsibility and does not take custody, the federal government will ensure that the person will not be released." Kagan also pointed out that, in reality, states typically do not volunteer to take custody of federal prisoners who are thought to be "sexually dangerous." In the end, the court held that the clause granted Congress sufficient authority to enact the Adam Walsh Protection and Safety Act.[20]

The terrorism statute was the focus of the 2010 case, *Holder v. Humanitarian Law Project*. Among the plaintiffs in the case were supporters of the Kurdistan Workers Party (KWP) and the Liberation Tigers of Tamil Eelam (LTTE); both groups engaged in both legal and illegal activities. Together, the two groups sought an injunction to prevent the government from enforcing sections of the Antiterrorism and Effective Death Penalty Act (AEDPA), Section 302, which authorized the Secretary of State to designate a group as a "foreign terrorist organization." Section 303 of the same act makes it a crime for anyone to provide "material support or resources" to even the nonviolent activities of a designated organization.[21]

Still, there were problems with the AEDPA; in previous cases, the courts ruled that Section 303 of the same act was unconstitutionally vague. In response, Congress passed the Intelligence Reform and Terrorism Prevention Act, which amended AEDPA. The new act added a "state of mind requirement," which stipulated that individuals must "knowingly" provide "material support or resources" in order to violate the Act. Congress also added terms to the Act that further clarified what constituted "material support or resources." The government moved for as summary judgment arguing that the challenged provisions of the AEDPA were not unconstitutionally vague. The district court then granted a partial motion for a summary judgment, but still held that some parts of the Act were unconstitutionally vague.

On appeal, the U.S. Court of Appeals for the Ninth Circuit affirmed, holding that the terms "service," "training," or "other specialized knowledge" within the AEDPA, as applied to the two plaintiffs, the KWP and the LTTE, were unconstitutionally vague. The question, then before the Supreme Court, was to decide whether the provisions of the AEDPA was constitutionally vague.[22]

In her opening argument, Kagan pointedly noted that the law is a vital one if the federal government is to be able to battle terrorism. But almost from the start, Kagan's defense was pummeled with hypothetical scenarios that the Justices put before her to test just how far her description of the material support law would reach. For instance, the newly appointed Justice Sonia Sotomayor questioned Kagan asking whether under the law an attorney representing a questionable group would be considered illegal support. Kagan said no, as if the group was charged with a crime, the group still had a constitutional right to defend itself, but also told the court, "To the extent the Court thinks some of these hypotheticals raise constitutional concerns, the Court can put those off to another day." That, however, did not stop the court from continuing to pose hypothetical scenarios to Kagan, to the point that Justice Ruth Bader Ginsburg queried just how Kagan was "drawing the line between legal and illegal support for a listed organization." Kagan's perseverance paid off; in the end, the court held that the material support provision of the AEDPA was constitutional as applied to those particular forms of support provided to terrorist organizations.[23]

CHANGE IN THE AIR

In her six appearances before the Supreme Court, Solicitor General Elena Kagan argued some of the most important and challenging constitutional tests to government action. Over the course of the 15 months she held the office, Kagan paid special attention to certain justices. For instance, Justice Anthony M. Kennedy, who often cast a deciding vote in the most close cases, was one that Kagan listened to quite intently, stating at one point that her fellow Harvard Law graduate possessed "independence and integrity." She enjoyed the verbal sparring with Justice Scalia. She also learned to accept help from Justice Ruth Bader Ginsburg, who once rephrased one of Kagan's arguments; to which Kagan said, "You said it better than I did, Justice Ginsburg."[24]

But relations between Kagan and the Chief Justice John G. Roberts Jr., seemed particularly sharp. Court watchers noted that Roberts, already known as a "sharp-edged questioner" particularly with those he disagreed with, appeared to be especially tough on Kagan. In one case, Roberts labeled one of Kagan's arguments "absolutely startling." Roberts also had been sharply critical of her legal reasoning. While some charged it to Roberts being hard on the person who now held the office he once held, others speculated if Robert's demeanor toward Kagan was harsh because Kagan had been mentioned as a potential nominee to the court.[25]

But by summer 2010, speculation about Kagan and the court suddenly became more than rumors and innuendo. For now, a new story was afoot: one of the justices was planning to retire and step down. If that were the case, then President Obama was being presented with another opportunity to place another justice on the nation's highest court.

NOTES

1. Nina Totenberg, "Solicitor General Kagan Holds Views Close to Her Chest," *NPR*, December 22, 2009, http://www.npr.org/templates/story/story.php?storyId=121712227.

2. Robert Barnes, "In Elena Kagan's Work as Solicitor General, Few Clues to Her Views," *Washington Post*, May 13, 2010, http://www.washingtonpost.com/wp-dyn/content/article/2010/05/12/AR2010051205049.html?sid=ST2010051300025.

3. Erin Miller, "Confirmation as Solicitor General," SCOTUS Blog, May 8, 2010, http://www.scotusblog.com/2010/05/9750-words-on-elena-kagan/.

4. Ibid.

5. Ibid.

6. Ibid.

7. Ibid.; Barnes, "In Elena Kagan's Work as Solicitor General, Few Clues to Her Views."

8. Miller, "Confirmation as Solicitor General."

9. Totenberg, "Solicitor General Kagan Holds Views Close to Her Chest."

10. Barnes, "In Elena Kagan's Work as Solicitor General, Few Clues to Her Views"; Totenberg, "Solicitor General Kagan Holds Views Close to Her Chest."

11. Bryan Garner, "Kagan's Teachers," *ABA Journal* 98, no. 9 (September 2012): 25–26.

12. Totenberg, "Solicitor General Kagan Holds Views Close to Her Chest."

13. Ibid.

14. Barnes, "In Elena Kagan's Work as Solicitor General, Few Clues to Her Views."

138 ELENA KAGAN

15. *Salazar v. Buono*, Oyez, 2009, http://www.oyez.org/cases/2000–2009/2009/2009_08_472.

16. Ibid.

17. Ibid.; Transcript: *Salazar v. Buono*, Supreme Court Website, 2009, http://www.supremecourt.gov/oral_arguments/argument_transcripts/08-472.pdf.

18. *United States v. Comstock*, Oyez, 2009, http://www.oyez.org/cases/2000–2009/2009/2009_08_1224.

19. Adam Liptak, "Supreme Court Weighs Authority, Not Legality, of Civil Confinements," *New York Times*, January 13, 2010, http://faculty.smu.edu/jkobylka/SCtItems/2009%20Term/Jan13-CivCommit.htm.

20. Ibid.

21. *Holder v. Humanitarian Law Project*, Oyez, n.d., http://www.oyez.org/cases/2000–2009/2009/2008_08_1498.

22. Ibid.

23. Lyle Denniston, "Analysis: Anti-terrorism Case Not An Easy One," *SCOTUS Blog*, February 23, 2010, http://www.scotusblog.com/2010/02/analysis-anti-terrorism-case-not-an-easy-one/.

24. Barnes, "In Elena Kagan's Work as Solicitor General, Few Clues to Her Views."

25. Ibid.

Chapter 10

JUSTICE KAGAN

April 9, 2010

My dear Mr. President:

Having concluded that it would be in the best interests of the Court to have my successor appointed and confirmed well in advance of the commencement of the Court's next Term, I shall retire from regular active service as an Associate Justice, under the provisions of 28 D.S.C. § 371(b), effective the next day after the Court rises for the summer recess this year.

Most respectfully yours,

John Paul Stevens[1]

THE SEARCH

With the announcement by Justice John Paul Stevens that he would step down from the Supreme Court bench, President Barack Obama found himself with a rare opportunity—to nominate and appoint back-to-back Supreme Court candidates during the first two years of his presidency. With the nomination and appointment of Justice Sonia Sotomayor just the year before, Obama was attempting to try and take the court away from its increasingly conservative bent. With the chance to place another of his choices on the bench, the president was given a tremendous opportunity to have a significant impact on the direction of the court, not just for years, but for decades. Further, the president hoped to have the new justice in place in time for the fall 2010 session.[2]

But the president also faced a formidable challenge: it was midterm election time and the Republican party was eager to shut down any candidate that appeared to be too liberal. The Democrats, even after having lost their 60-vote supermajority in the Senate, were also eager for a fight. Gone were the days when bipartisanship came into play during the nomination and confirmation process. "No matter who he sends up," said the leader of a liberal group, "Republicans are loaded for bear and will oppose."[3]

THE TOP THREE

Even though rumors had been circulating about a possible retirement from the Supreme Court, the announcement by Justice Stevens left many scrambling to decide what names the candidate pool might include. In all, the president was considering 10 names, with 3 names already being touted as the leading candidates. But all the dossiers in front of the president illustrated a wide range of backgrounds, ideology, and experience. The battle for confirmation would in large part be shaped by whomever the president picked.[4]

Among the top three candidates under consideration by the president was Merrick B. Garland, an appeals court judge in Washington, D.C. According to political and legal analysts, Garland was considered to be the safest choice of the president's potential candidates meaning that the chances of a potential confrontation with the Republicans would be relatively low. Garland was well-liked in the legal community where many viewed him as "kind of Democratic version of Chief Justice John G. Roberts Jr."[5] Diane P. Wood, a federal appeals court judge in Chicago, was considered to be the most liberal of the top three candidates and had been on Obama's short list the year before. A divorced mother of three, Wood's "real-life experience" was considered a valuable political commodity by the president. A possible roadblock to her nomination was Wood's strong stand on abortion rights, something that conservatives would not favor and something that the president had to weigh carefully. But the fact was Wood's strong support for abortion rights would provoke a confrontation with conservatives. One antiabortion group, Americans United for Life, had already warned that Wood's nomination "would return the abortion wars to the Supreme Court."[6]

The remaining top-three choice was Elena Kagan. Once again, her potential shortcomings were trotted out in the media—the lack of scholarly writings, and her never having been a judge. Despite her work as solicitor general, many believed that Kagan was not Supreme Court material. Because of her scant trail of scholarly writing, many were concerned that little was known about Kagan's views on the most pressing issues of the day. But, Kagan was also considered to be the top favorite of the president; her relative youth—she was only 50 years old—also meant that she could have a considerable impact on the court for decades.[7]

MOVING QUICKLY

In the following days, the president promised to move quickly in announcing a nominee; however, White House senior advisers said it could take several weeks before a decision was to be reached. In speaking with the press, the president offered that he was looking for a candidate that possessed qualities similar to the departing Justice Stevens, in that the nominee would have "an independent mind, a record of excellence and integrity, a fierce dedication to the rule of law and a keen understanding of how the law affects the daily lives of the American people." The president also added that the new justice would be a person who knows that "In a democracy, powerful interests must not be allowed to drown out the voices of ordinary citizens." As one White House advisor commented later, "I think that in choosing a Supreme Court justice the president is less likely to compromise and more likely to go with his heart than on any other matter."[8]

Helping President Obama with the decision-making process was a Supreme Court nomination team. The group was headed up by White House counsel, Robert F. Bauer, and overseen by the president's chief of staff, Rahn Emanuel. Once a nominee was picked, Bauer's wife, Anita Dunn, President Obama's former communications director, would co-ordinate with advocacy groups. Finally, Vice President Biden would also be helping with the process.[9]

Working with his team during the selection process, the president reviewed the writings of all the potential candidates. From a list of 20 names, 10 were chosen; then, more research was done on each of the 10 candidates. In addition, the president and vice president spoke with four of the candidates personally, including Kagan and Wood. For both women, it was a repeat performance of the previous year when both were interviewed for the open seat on the bench that eventually went to Sonia Sotomayor. Interestingly, several Senators spoke to the president about the possibility of a nominee that was not a judge—someone, in fact, like Kagan. Said one White House advisor, "If you took the position that someone with her [Kagan's] kind of experience couldn't serve on the Supreme Court, then you would have a situation where Thurgood Marshall would never have served on the Supreme Court and Robert Jackson would have never served on the Supreme Court."[10]

THE WORST KEPT SECRET

On May 17, 2010, President Obama met with reporters in the East Room of the White House to announce what was currently considered the worst kept secret: his nominee for the Supreme Court. After giving a few remarks about the retiring Justice Stevens, Obama then introduced the nominee, "his friend" Elena Kagan:

Elena is widely regarded as one of the nation's foremost legal minds. She's an acclaimed legal scholar with a rich understanding of constitutional law. . . . And she has won accolades from observers across the ideological spectrum for her well-reasoned arguments and commanding presence.

But Elena is respected and admired not just for her intellect and record of achievement, but also for her temperament—her openness to a broad array of viewpoints; her habit, to borrow a phrase from Justice Stevens, "of understanding before disagreeing"; her fair-mindedness and skill as a consensus-builder.[11]

The president, also drawing on Kagan's background as a New Yorker, joked, "This appreciation for diverse views may also come in handy as a die-hard Mets fan serving alongside her new colleague-to-be, Yankees fan Justice Sotomayor, who I believe has ordered a pinstriped robe for the occasion," which prompted laughter from the audience.[12]

When it came time for her to speak, Kagan made a point of thanking her mentors and her staff. She also thanked her brothers and then her parents, whom were no longer living:

I'm thankful to my brothers and other family and friends for coming to Washington to be with me here today. And much more,

Solicitor General Elena Kagan being introduced as the president's choice for Supreme Court Justice in Washington, D.C. (Official White House Photo by Lawrence Jackson)

I am thankful for all of their support and loyalty and love, not just on this day but always. . . . If this day has just a touch of sadness in it for me, it is because my parents aren't here to share it. They were both, as the President said, the children of immigrants and the first in their families to go to college. . . . My parents' lives and their memory remind me every day of the impact public service can have, and I pray every day that I live up to the example they set.[13]

Kagan also talked about the opportunity awaiting her as a potential Supreme Court justice, saying, "The court is an extraordinary institution in the work it does and in the work it can do for the American people by advancing the tenets of our Constitution, by upholding the rule of law and by enabling all Americans, regardless of their background or their beliefs, to get a fair hearing and an equal chance at justice."

After the announcement, a briefing was held in which a top adviser to Vice President Biden, who had been working on the nomination, stated that in all likelihood Kagan would step down from her duties as solicitor general duties immediately, and then begin the arduous process of reaching out to senators in order to court votes. One potential downside to Kagan's nomination and confirmation was the fact that, if confirmed, her past work for the Obama administration would force her to recuse herself from as many as 17 Supreme Court cases over the next two years.[14]

BOTH SIDES SPEAK OUT

Even before the White House made its formal announcement, critics of Kagan were already sharpening their knives. A law professor at the University of Colorado, writing on *The Daily Beast*, compared Kagan to Harriet E. Miers, the Supreme Court nominee of President George W. Bush, whose nomination collapsed when conservatives charged that Miers was unqualified and not favorably disposed to their particular brand of judicial philosophy. Another critic, who served as the president of the Ethics and Public Policy Center in Washington, wrote on *National Review*'s Web site that even Kagan's nonjudicial experience was inadequate, remarking: "Kagan may well have less experience relevant to the work of being a justice than any entering justice in decades."[15]

Not all liberals were in the Kagan camp either. Many were wary of Kagan for many of the same reasons as conservative critics were: no one really knew where she stood on important issues. Because there was no public record of her thinking, it was hard to predict how Kagan might respond as a member of the Supreme Court. Wrote one liberal legal blogger: "Nothing is a better fit for this White House than a blank slate, institution-loyal, seemingly principle-free careerist who spent the last 15 months as the Obama administration's lawyer vigorously defending every one of his assertions of extremely broad executive authority." The left-leaning publication *The Nation* was also skeptical, stating, "The truth is, on the fundamental issues of executive power and civil liberties, we simply do not know enough about Kagan's views; because she was never a judge and has a relatively slim paper trail as a scholar and a litigator (in which her role was constrained), we are left parsing these few statements for larger meaning." The editors then went on to say:

> Kagan should be pressed on all these matters during her confirmation hearing. Will she get the serious discussion and substantive debate that she once advocated for all Supreme Court nominees? That depends on two things. Will Senate Democrats exercise their duty to review the nominee independently, or will they defer to the president out of expediency, ensuring what Kagan once lamented as the "safest and surest route to the prize"? And will Senate Republicans allow such debate to take place, or will they make a mockery of the process and take the line of attack already fomenting on right-wing websites—whisper campaigns about her personal life, unsubstantiated assertions that she is a "stealth radical" and unsupportable claims that she is underqualified ("the Left's Harriet Miers")?[16]

Kagan's former boss, Bill Clinton, was an enthusiastic supporter of Kagan's nomination. In an interview, Clinton said, "Working in the White House exposed Kagan to a lot of things," which was good in his opinion. "You want somebody on the court who is really smart and knows the law and understands it. But you also want somebody who cares about the impact of the decisions they make on ordinary people. Will this law change the lives of people, and if so, how?" As for the concerns from the left that Kagan might be too much a centrist and not able to stand up to the conservative elements on the court, Clinton agreed that Kagan was not a liberal, in the sense that Thurgood Marshall or William J. Brennan were. Still, Clinton stood by his former lawyer, remarking: "I think she is really sort of a common-sense progressive," he said. "I think she has good liberal values, but she is also immensely practical, and I think she will be fair to both parties."[17]

There was also some humor to be found in the wake of Kagan's nomination. Jay Horowitz, the spokesman for the New York Mets baseball team, told a report of the *New York Times* "that the team did not know it had such a fan in such a high place." Further, the Mets were very proud that Kagan was a fan. The article also went on to say that some Mets fans were not going to wait for the confirmation hearings or the Senate vote and were asking if Kagan "can push for a constitutional challenge to the reign of Omar Minaya [the then general manager of the team]."[18]

In the meantime, Kagan made her way to the Senate where she paid one-on-one calls to the senators. She was always accompanied by a small group of White House aides, including Associate White House Counsel Susan Davies, Legislative Affairs aide Christopher Kang, and often one or two others of the president's lawyers and strategists. Their job was to take notes of any exchanges between Kagan and the senators; the task was two-fold: one, to help Kagan prepare for her confirmation hearings, and two, to make sure that any private utterance is noted in case anyone tried to misconstrue a remark Kagan made to a senator later. In addition, the White House was also working with the Clinton Presidential Library in Little Rock, Arkansas, to release tens of thousands of pages of files from Kagan's time as an aide to the former president. The library made the records available every Friday afternoon over a three-week period.[19]

Even as liberals and conservatives were lining up and weighing in on Kagan, the American public was not so quick to form an opinion. In the week before Kagan's confirmation hearings were to get underway, an Associated Press-Gallup Poll found that 63 percent of Americans polled said they haven't heard enough about Kagan to form a good or bad opinion of her; another 43 percent thought Kagan should be confirmed, with 26 percent saying that Kagan should not be confirmed. Compared to Sonia Sotomayor's poll numbers, taken at roughly the same time a year before, Sotomayor had enjoyed a stronger public backing—with 50 percent of the Americans polled supporting her nomination—in spite of the fact that Sotomayor was a much more controversial figure. The current news climate also helped deflect news about the Kagan nomination; with more Americans concerned about the economy, the horrific oil spill in the Gulf of Mexico, and midterm elections, the debate over Kagan's fitness for the court was considerably more muted.[20]

The White House also worked overtime to keep the more controversial aspects of Kagan's nomination in the background, while playing up others of her life, such as it was. Compared to Sotomayor, Kagan, her family, and friends maintained a very tight-lipped response to questions about her life, often refusing to answer media queries at all. In addition, White House aides let few criticism of Kagan sit for very long and made a point of contacting the press as soon as any kind of critical comment was made about Kagan.[21]

THE HEARINGS

On Monday, June 28, 2010, the confirmation hearings finally got underway. In a curious beginning to the hearings, Republican senators began by pushing Kagan on how her legal views mirrored those of Justice Thurgood Marshall, whom Kagan clerked for. As one reporter noted, "You might have thought Marshall himself was before the Senate," given the tone of the questions put to Kagan. For example, Senator John Kyl of Arizona offered his opinion that Marshall's judicial philosophy "is not what I would consider to be mainstream," while Senator Jeff Sessions of Alabama called the landmark civil right attorney and justice "a well-known activist." Senator Chuck Grassley stated he found Marshall's legal view to "not comport with the proper role of a judge or judicial method." Senator John Cornyn described Marshall "a judicial activist" with a "judicial philosophy that concerns me." Further, it was pointed out that Marshall believed the death penalty unconstitutional, supported abortion rights, and was a strong proponent of judicial activism. At this point, Kagan reminded the senators that if confirmed "you will get Justice Kagan. You won't get Justice Marshall."[22]

One reporter for the *Washington Post* quipped:

> With Kagan's confirmation hearings expected to last most of
> the week, Republicans may still have time to make cases against
> Nelson Mandela, Mother Teresa and Gandhi. . . . The problem
> with this line of attack is that Marshall was already confirmed
> by the Senate—in 1967. He died in 1993.

Certainly, one member of the audience that was puzzled by the tack in
the Republicans' questioning was Marshall's son, Thurgood "Goody"
Marshall Jr., who sat two rows behind Kagan, and "listened with amuse-
ment" to the assaults on his father. Marshall later said, "I was a little
surprised. . . . He [his father] would've probably had the same reaction
I did: It's time to talk about Elena." But as the reporter noted, "Talking
about Elena is boring."[23]

It was clear to many in the audience that the committee had no clear
line of attack against Kagan. as illustrated by Senator Cornyn's opening statement when he referred to a quotation that he received in an
email: "Liberty is not a cruise ship full of pampered passengers. Liberty
is a man of war, and we're all the crew." "I don't know why I thought
of that," Cornyn told the perplexed audience. Kagan did not help matters either with her beginning statement which was deemed "vapid,"
"banal," and was read so slowly that a "bipartisan wave of yawns and
eye-rubbing hit the dais."[24]

By the second day of the hearings, it was clear that Kagan was actually enjoying the lecturing and goading from her Republican interro-
gators, and as one reporter noted, "She *loves this stuff.* . . . She comes
alive." As the reporter described the hearings:

> Over two days at the microphone, Kagan gave the impression that
> there was no place she would rather be than seeking to address all
> questions of the members of the Senate Judiciary Committee. She
> assured even the openly hostile Republican members that she
> knows they are men of "good faith." And when the Democrats
> grumbled about the court under Chief Justice John G. Roberts
> Jr., she enthusiastically responded that he, too, certainly is a man
> of "good faith." She was expansive on the question of whether a

judge is an umpire (in some ways), a robot (never), an ideologue (so wrong) or an empath (certainly not).

At times, the candidate was even folksy, refusing to "count her chickens" before hatching when Senator Arlen Specter tried to get Kagan to speculate how she might rule on an issue before the court. When Kagan needed time to come up with an answer, she did not fidget or stumble, but instead said "gosh." Other times, she cracked jokes. As one article later described the scene, "Kagan displayed such relish and expertise at the hearing table that she could hire herself out as a stunt witness and work five days a week on Capitol Hill."[25]

Over the course of the hearings, Republican committee members hammered at Kagan. She was questioned about her decision to ban military recruiters from the school's office of career services, when she was dean of the Harvard Law School. Kagan replied that the military enjoyed full access to the campus; however, members of the committee said Kagan's statement was false, and that federal law required campuses to allow recruiters full access, not some access, as they had at Harvard. Further, she was accused of trying to advance her own agenda against the "don't ask, don't' tell" policy. In addition, Republicans also expressed concerns over how Kagan might rule on cases involving issues dear to conservatives: gun rights, property rights, abortion, and the scope of congressional power.[26]

Kagan agreed with the committee that her politics tended to be "progressive," but also hastened to add that her personal beliefs would have no bearing on her rulings. Further, Kagan stated that her decisions were not a projection of personal beliefs or values, but that she was representing an institution, whether it was the Harvard Law School, the White House, or the federal government. At one point, Senator Herb Kohl asked Kagan why she even wanted to be a justice of the Supreme Court; in fact, it took Kohl five tries before he finally got Kagan to answer the question:

That's, I think, the right way for a judge to do a job, is one case at a time, thinking about the case fairly and objectively and impartially. And in—in the course of doing that, of course, people's lives change, because law has an effect on people. And you hope very much that law improves people's lives and has a beneficial effect on our society. That's the entire purpose of law.[27]

In the end, it was much ado about nothing. By Wednesday, after some 17 hours of grilling, Kagan's critics were beaming at her. At one point, Senator Tom Coburn told her, "I know this hasn't been the most pleasant experience for you," and even telling Kagan that she lit up the room. Kagan responded by telling the committee, "I think it's been terrific, that everybody has been very fair and very considerate, and I hope you found it informative. I found it somewhat wearying, but actually a great moment in my life."[28]

CONFIRMED!

On August 5, 2010, the Senate met to vote on whether or not to confirm Elena Kagan as the 112th Supreme Court Justice of the United States. Despite the firm opposition mounted by the Republican members of the Judiciary Committee and also from Republicans on the Senate floor, Kagan won a relatively easy confirmation. There was no filibuster from the Republican side of the aisle and the vote for the most part broke down along party lines. The final vote was 68–31; five Republicans voted for her and one Democrat against her. The vote was identical to that of President Obama's nominee the prior year—Sonia Sotomayor.[29]

Prior to the voting, Senate majority leader Harry Reid elaborated on his reasons for supporting Kagan's nomination: "Because of her intellect and integrity; her reason, restraint, and respect for the rule of law; her unimpeachable character and unwavering fidelity to our Constitution, I am proud to cast my vote for her confirmation." Senate minority leader Mitch McConnell also had his moment in stating why Kagan should not be given a seat on the nation's highest court: "Ms. Kagan's background as a political operative, her lengthy resume of zealous advocacy for political and ideological causes, often at the expense of the law and those whose views differ from her own, her attachment to the president and his political and ideological goals, including his belief in the extraconstitutional notion that judges should favor some over others make her precisely the kind of nominee, in my view, the Founders were concerned about and that senators would have reason to oppose."

On Saturday, August 7, 2010, Elena Kagan, wearing a dark grey suit, was sworn into office by Chief Justice Roberts. Placing her left hand on a bible, Kagan promised to "administer justice without respect to persons and do equal right to the poor and to the rich." In October, there would be another ceremony marking her confirmation, shortly before the fall session of the court got underway.

Elena Kagan's confirmation to the Supreme Court was filled with historic firsts. When the court convened in October, it would mark the first time three women would serve together as justices, as Kagan joined Sonia Sotomayor and Ruth Bader Ginsburg. Kagan will also be the youngest member of the court. Until then, there will be some uncertainty by those who opposed Kagan's nomination. Perhaps, the biggest question was what kind of justice will Kagan be? Will she chart a moderate course among the court or will she push through a more liberal agenda that closely follows the president's? For President Obama, the victory was sweet; he called Kagan's confirmation "a sign of progress that I relish not just as a father who wants limitless possibilities for my two daughters, but as an American proud that our Supreme Court will be more inclusive, more representative and more reflective of us as a people than ever before."[30]

For Elena Kagan, the rise to the highest court in the land is nothing more than the realization of a long ago dream made while in high

The newest Supreme Court Justice: Elena Kagan. (Steve Petteway, Collection of the Supreme Court of the United States)

school. Her journey, while marked by many successes, was not without its disappointments and setbacks. There is also a poignancy about Kagan's success story; in the end, her mother wanted nothing more than for her to be married while her father did not live to see her achieve her goal of ascending to the bench of the Supreme Court. For all the criticism about Kagan and her seeming inability to state her views, she has only done what she set out to do—her job—whether as a lawyer for the White House, the dean of the Harvard Law School, or solicitor general for the United States. She is someone who has done that job well; and she did it without letting personal views hamper or intrude on the task that needed to be done. It is this same quality that will carry Elena Kagan as she makes her way in a new role: as Supreme Court Justice, in which she will continue to strive to serve her country in the best way possible.

NOTES

1. John Paul Stevens, "Resignation Letter," CSPAN, 2010, http://www.c-span.org/pdf/stevens040910.pdf.

2. Sheryl Gay Stolberg and Charlie Savage, "Stevens's Retirement Is Political Test for Obama," *New York Times*, April 9, 2010, http://www.nytimes.com/2010/04/10/us/politics/10stevens.html.

3. Ibid.

4. Ibid.

5. Ibid.

6. Ibid.

7. Ibid.

8. Ibid.

9. Ibid.

10. Michael Scherer, "Court Nominee Elena Kagan: Let the Scrutiny Start," *Time*, May 10, 2010, http://www.time.com/time/politics/article/0,8599,1988179,00.html.

11. Jesse Lee, "Nominating Kagan: Her Passion for the Law is Anything but Academic," *New York Times*, May 10, 2010, http://www.whitehouse.gov/blog/2010/05/10/nominating-kagan-her-passion-law-anything-academic.

12. Ibid.

13. Ibid.

14. Ibid.

15. Peter Baker and Jeff Zelany, "Obama Picks Kagan, Scholar but Not Judge, for Court Seat," *New York Times*, May 10, 2010, http://www.nytimes.com/2010/05/11/us/politics/11court.html?pagewanted=all.

16. Scherer, "Court Nominee Elena Kagan"; "Judging Elena Kagan," *Nation*, May 31, 2010, http://www.thenation.com/article/judging-elena-kagan#.

17. Carl Hulse, "Bill Clinton Speaks Out on Court Nominee, Recalling Her Service in White House," *New York Times*, June 20, 2010, Section A, p. 23.

18. James Barron, "Obama's Plan to Balance the Bench (Mets vs. Yankees)," *New York Times*, May 10, 2010, http://cityroom.blogs.nytimes.com/2010/05/10/obamas-plan-to-balance-the-bench-mets-vs-yankees/.

19. Julie Hirschfield Davis, "White House Choreographs Dance towards Supreme Court Confirmation," *Cleveland Plain Dealer*, June 17, 2010, http://www.cleveland.com/nation/index.ssf/2010/06/white_house_choreographs_elena.html.

20. Ibid.

21. Ibid.

22. Dana Milbank, "Kagan May Get Confirmed, but Thurgood Marshall Can Forget It," *Washington Post*, June 29, 2010, http://www.washingtonpost.com/wp-dyn/content/article/2010/06/28/AR2010062805129.html.

23. Ibid.

24. Ibid.

25. Ann Gerhart, "At Hearings, Elena Kagan Charmed Her Critics—and Seemed to Enjoy Herself," *Washington Post*, June 30, 2010, http://www.washingtonpost.com/wp-dyn/content/article/2010/06/30/AR2010063005254.html?sid=ST2010062802981.

26. Warren Richey, "Elena Kagan Confirmed to Supreme Court," *CSMonitor*, August 5, 2010, http://www.csmonitor.com/USA/Politics/2010/0805/Elena-Kagan-confirmed-to-Supreme-Court.

27. Ann Gerhart, "At Hearings, Elena Kagan Charmed Her Critics—and Seemed to Enjoy Herself."

28. Ibid.

29. Richey, "Elena Kagan Confirmed to Supreme Court."

30. Carl Hulse, "Senate Confirms Kagan in Partisan Vote," *New York Times*, August 6, 2010, http://www.nytimes.com/2010/08/06/us/politics/06kagan.html?_r=0.

BIBLIOGRAPHY

Associated Press. "160,000 Docs Released from Clinton Library Reveal Elana Kagan Favors Politics over Policy." *New York Daily News*, June 19, 2010, http://www.nydailynews.com/news/politics/160–000-docs-released-clinton-library-reveal-elana-kagan-favors-politics-policy-article-1.180715.

Baker, Peter, and Jeff Zelany. "Obama Picks Kagan, Scholar but Not Judge, for Court Seat." *New York Times*, May 10, 2010, http://www.nytimes.com/2010/05/11/us/politics/11court.html?pagewanted=all.

Barnes, Robert. "High Court Nominee Never Let Lack of Experience Hold Her Back." *Washington Post*, May 10, 2010, p. A05.

Barnes, Robert. "In Elena Kagan's Work as Solicitor General, Few Clues to Her Views." *Washington Post*, May 13, 2010, http://www.washingtonpost.com/wp-dyn/content/article/2010/05/12/AR2010051205049.html?sid=ST2010051300025.

Barron, James. "Obama's Plan to Balance the Bench (Mets vs. Yankees)." *New York Times*, May 10, 2010, http://cityroom.blogs.nytimes.com/2010/05/10/obamas-plan-to-balance-the-bench-mets-vs-yankees/.

Bell, Derrick. "The Supreme Court 1984 Term: The Civil Rights Chronicles." *Harvard Law Review*, November 1985, 99. Harv.L.Rev.4, http://www.lexisnexis.com.ezproxy2.rmc.edu/hottopics/lnacademic/?.

Blau, Reuvan Blau. "Ford to City: Drop Dead: President's Snub Inspired, Not Discouraged, Ex-Gov. Hugh Carey." *NY Daily News*, August 8, 2011, http://articles.nydailynews.com/2011–08–08/news/29882248_1_felix-rohatyn-president-ford-unions.

Bravin, Jess. "Kagan Worked On Jones Lawsuit for Clinton." *Wall Street Journal*, June 12, 2010, http://online.wsj.com/article/SB100014240527487035094045753003826096 56828.html.

Bravin, Jess. "Justice Kagan Pens First Opinion, an 8–1 Win for Credit Card Companies." *Wall Street Journal*, January 11, 2011, http://blogs.wsj.com/law/2011/01/11/justice-kagan-pens-first-opinion-an-8–1-win-for-credit-card-companies/.

Caplan, Lincoln. "The Talented Justice Kagan." *New York Times*, June 29, 2013, http://www.nytimes.com/2013/06/30/opinion/sunday/the-talented-justice-kagan.html?ref=kaganelena.

Chambers, Christopher. "Elena Kagan Is No Thurgood Marshall." *Grio*, May 11, 2010, http://thegrio.com/2010/05/11/why-elena-kagan-is-no-thurgood-marshall/.

"The Changing Faces of First Amendment Neutrality: *R.A. V v. St. Paul, Rust v. Sullivan*, and the Problem of Content-Based Underinclusion." *Supreme Court Review* 29, 1992.

Cliatt, Cass. "Princeton Alumna Kagan Nominated to Supreme Court." *News at Princeton*, May 10, 2010, http://www.princeton.edu/main/news/archive/S27/34/66S12/index.xml?section=top stories.

Cook, Blanche Weisen. "Bella Azbug," 1998–2013, http://www.jewishvirtuallibrary.org/jsource/biography/abzug.html.

Daly, Michael. "Educated in School and on City's Streets." *New York Daily News*, May 11, 2010, p. 6.

Davis, Julie Hirschfield. "White House Choreographs Dance towards Supreme Court Confirmation." *Cleveland Plain Dealer*, June 17, 2010, http://www.cleveland.com/nation/index.ssf/2010/06/white_house_choreographs_elena.html.

Denniston, Lyle. "Analysis: Anti-Terrorism Case Not An Easy One." *SCOTUS Blog*, February 23, 2010, http://www.scotusblog.com/2010/02/analysis-anti-terrorism-case-not-an-easy-one/.

Doyle, Michael. "Kagan's Courtroom Career Includes Brushes with Rappers," 2010, http://www.mcclatchydc.com/2010/05/13/94119/kagans-courtroom-career-includes.html#.UZKUu6KcHwM.

"Elena Kagan. Biography." Bio. True Story, 2010, http://www.biography.com/people/elena-kagan-560228.

"Elena Kagan: Cub Reporter." *Daily Beast*, May 19, 2010, http://www.thedailybeast.com/newsweek/2010/05/19/elena-kagan-cub-reporter.html.

"Elena Kagan." *News Media & the Law* 34, no. 2 (Spring 2010): 29–25.

"Elena Kagan's College Years: At Princeton She Was Both 'Vivacious' and Reserved." *Huffington Post*, May 5, 2010, http://www.huffingtonpost.com/2010/05/05/elena-kagans-college-year_n_564894.html.

"Elena Kagan: Supreme Court Nominee Has Taken Doctrinal Approach to Free-Speech and Free-Press Issues." *News Media & the Law.* Spring 2010, p. 21.

"Firm Overview." Williams & Connolly LLC website, 2013, http://www.wc.com/about.html.

Foderaro, Lisa. "Growing Up, Kagan Tested Boundaries of Her Faith." *New York Times*, May 12, 2010, http://www.nytimes.com/2010/05/13/nyregion/13synagogue.html?_r=0.

Foderaro, Lisa, and Christine Haughney. "The Kagan Family: Left-Leaning and Outspoken." *New York Times*, June 18, 2010, p. MB1.

Galer, Sarah. "Former Professor Elena Kagan Nominated to Supreme Court." *University of Chicago News Office*, May 10, 2010, http://www.law.uchicago.edu/node/2998.

Garner, Bryan. "Kagan's Teachers." *ABA Journal* 98, no. 9 (September 2012): 25–26.

Gerhart, Ann. "At hearings, Elena Kagan Charmed Her Critics—and Seemed to Enjoy Herself." *Washington Post*, June 30, 2010, http://www.washingtonpost.com/wp-dyn/content/article/2010/06/30/AR2010063005254.html?sid=ST2010062802981.

Gerstein, Josh. "As Harvard Seeks a President, Dean Kagan's Star Is Rising." *New York Sun*, March 10, 2006, http://www.nysun.com/national/as-harvard-seeks-a-president-dean-kagans-star-is/28925/.

Goldstein, Amy, Carol D. Leonnig, and Peter Slevin. "For Supreme Court Nominee Elena Kagan, a History of Pragmatism over Partisanship." *Washington Post*, May 11, 2010, http://www.washington post.com/wp-dyn/content/article/2010/05/10/AR2010051002787 .html?sid=ST2010080505264.

Goldstein, Amy, Carol D. Leonnig, and Peter Slevin. "Kagan, as Harvard Law School Dean, Pursued Two Courses on 'Don't Ask' Policy." *Washington Post*, May 28, 2010, http://www.washingtonpost.com/ wp-dyn/content/article/2010/05/27/AR2010052705686.html.

Greenwald, Glenn. "Justice Stevens' Retirement and Elena Kagan: One of the Potential Front-Runners, Obama's Solicitor general, Would Shift the Supreme Court to the Right." *Salon*, April 9, 2010, http://www.salon.com/2010/04/09/stevens_6/.

Harvard Law School. "History." Harvard Law School. Webpage last updated October 2012, http://www.law.harvard.edu/about/history .html.

Hinz, Greg. "Ab Mikva Talks about His Ex-Clerk, Elena Kagan." *Crain's Chicago Business*, May 10, 2010, http://www.chicagobusiness.com/ article/20100510/BLOGS02/305109993/ab-mikva-talks-about-his-ex-clerk-elena-kagan.

Hulse, Carl. "Bill Clinton Speaks Out on Court Nominee, Recalling Her Service in White House." *New York Times*, June 20, 2010, Section A, p. 23.

Hulse, Carl. "Senate Confirms Kagan in Partisan Vote." *New York Times*, August 6, 2010, http://www.nytimes.com/2010/08/06/us/politics/ 06kagan.html?_r=0.

Kagan, Elena. "Curriculim Vitae." *Washington Post*, http://www.washing tonpost.com/wp-srv/politics/documents/KaganCorrespondence .pdf.

Kagan, Elena. "Application for Justice Marshall Clerkship." February 19, 1986, http://www.paperlessarchives.com/ElenaKaganDocuments A22.pdf.

Kagan, Elena. "Confirmation Messes, Old and New." *University of Chicago Law Review* 919, no. 62 (1995): 934–36.

Kagan, Elena. "The Development and Erosion of the American Exclusionary Rule: A Study in Judicial Method." Oxford University, June 1983, p. 44, http://online.wsj.com/public/resources/documents/kagan1983thesis.pdf.

Kagan, Elena. "Foreword." In *Transformations in American Legal History: Essays in Honor of Professor Morton J. Horwitz*, edited by Daniel Hamilton and Alfred Brophy. Cambridge: Harvard University, 2009, pp. v–viii.

Kagan, Elena. "In Memoriam: Clark Byse." *Harvard Law Review* 454, no. 121 (2007): 453–454

Kagan, Elena. "In Memoriam: David Westfall." *Harvard Law Review* 947, no. 119 (2006): 947–948.

Kagan, Elena. "In Memoriam: Thurgood Marshall." *Texas Law Review*, May 1993—71 Tex. L. Rev. 1125, p. 1125.

Kagan, Lupic, Lepper Finklestein & Gold: Attorneys at Law, http://www.kll-law.com/bio-wlubic.asp.

Kreps, Daniel. "Why the Once-Controversial Rap Group Is Throwing Its Support Behind the Supreme Court Justice Nominee." *Rolling Stone*, July 8, 2010, http://www.rollingstone.com/music/news/elena-kagans-biggest-supporter-2-live-crew-20100708.

Lee, Carol. "Gay Rights Central to Kagan Fight." *Politico*, May 12, 2010, http://www.politico.com/news/stories/0510/37110.html.

Lee, Jesse. "Nominating Kagan: Her Passion for the Law Is Anything But Academic." *New York Times*, May 10, 2010, http://www.whitehouse.gov/blog/2010/05/10/nominating-kagan-her-passion-law-anything-academic.

"Liptak, Adam. "Obama's Choice for Solicitor General Has Left a Breach in a Long Paper Trail." *New York Times*, January 7, 2009, Section A, p. 15.

Liptak, Adam. "Supreme Court Weighs Authority, Not Legality, of Civil Confinements." *New York Times*, January 13, 2010, http://faculty.smu.edu/jkobylka/SCtItems/2009%20Term/Jan13-CivCommit.htm.

Liptak, Adam. "Kagan's View of the Court Confirmation Process, before She Was a Part of It." *New York Times*, May 11, 2010, http://www.nytimes.com/2010/05/12/us/politics/12court.html?pagewanted=all.

Liptak, Adam, and Sheryl Gay Stolberg. "Kagan's E-Mail at Clinton White House Reveals a Blunt, Savvy Legal Adviser." *New York Times*, June 18, 2010, http://www.nytimes.com/2010/06/19/us/politics/19kagan.html?_r=0.

Liptak, Adam. "Bound Together on the Court, but by Beliefs, Not Gender." *New York Times*, July 1, 2013, http://www.nytimes.com/2013/07/02/us/bound-together-on-the-court-but-by-beliefs-not-gender.html?ref=kaganelena&_r=0.

Lithwick, Dahlia. "Her Honor." *New York* 44, no. 40 (2010):. 46–51.

MacGinnis, Alec. "Elena Kagan Has Been Battle Tested by Tobacco Legislation in the '90s." *Washington Post*, June 4, 2010, http://www.washingtonpost.com/wp-dyn/content/article/2010/06/03/AR2010060303536.html.

Mascarenhas, Rohan. "U.S. Supreme Court Nominee Elena Kagan's Writings, Views While at Princeton to Be Examined Published: Monday." *The Star-Ledger*, May 10, 2010, http://www.nj.com/news/index.ssf/2010/05/us_supreme_court_nominee_elena.

McLaughlin, Seth. "Administration Lost Two-Thirds of Rulings." *Washington Times*, June 27, 2013, Section A, p. 1.

Mears, Bill. "Kagan Documents Reveal Role in Whitewater Negotiations." *CNN.Politics*, June 11, 2012, http://www.cnn.com/2010/POLITICS/06/11/scotus.kagan.documents/index.html.

Meckler, Laura. "Grading Kagan as Dean: Kagan Built Bridges on Divided Campus, but Other Factors Helped Her Along." *Wall Street Journal*, May 12, 2010, http://online.wsj.com/article/SB10001424052748703565804575238740862226702.html.

Merrill, Robert. "A Veteran's Harvard Ally: Elena Kagan." *Washington Post*, May 21, 2010, http://www.washingtonpost.com/wp-dyn/content/article/2010/05/20/AR2010052003940.html.

Milbank, Dana. "Wonderwonk." *New Republic*, May 18, 1998, http://www.newrepublic.com/article/politics/wonderwonk#.

Milbank, Dana. "Kagan May Get Confirmed, but Thurgood Marshall Can Forget It." *Washington Post*, June 29, 2010, http://www.washingtonpost.com/wp-dyn/content/article/2010/06/28/AR2010062805129.html.

Miller, Erin. "Confirmation as Solicitor General." *SCOTUS Blog*, May 8, 2010,: http://www.scotusblog.com/2010/05/9750-words-on-elena-kagan/.

Miller, Janet. "Supreme Court Justice Elena Kagan Tells U-M Crowd about Serious and Not-So-Serious Workings of the High Court." *AnnArbor.com*, September 7, 2012, http://www.annarbor.com/ne ws/supreme-court-justice-elena-kagan-discusses-the-serious-and-not-so-serious-workings-of-the-high-cour/.

Milligan, Susan. "Personal Ties Bind Obama, Kagan." *Boston Globe*, May 16, 2010, http://www.boston.com/news/nation/washington/articles/2010/05/16/personal_ties_bind_obama_kagan/.

Mordfin, Robin I. "From the Green Lounge to the White House." University of Chicago Law School, n.d., http://www.law.uchi cago.edu/alumni/magazine/spring09/greenloungetowhite house.

Mystal, Elie. "Elena Kagan and Me: One Semester of Civ Pro with the New SCOTUS Nominee." *Above the Law*, n.d., http://abovethe law.com/2010/05/elena-kagan-and-me-one-semester-of-civ-pro-with-the-new-scotus-nominee/.

"New York City Blackout, 1977." http://blackout.gmu.edu/events/tl1977 .html.

Obituary. "Robert Kagan 67, Lawyer for Tenants." *New York Times*, July 25, 1994, http://www.nytimes.com/1994/07/25/obituaries/ro bert-kagan-67-lawyer-for-tenants.html.

Otterman, Sharon. "Court Pick Can Still Rise on Her High School Alumni's List." *New York Times*, May 10, 2010, http://www.ny times.com/2010/05/11/nyregion/11hunter.html.

Pareles, Jon. "An Album is Judged Obscene; Rap: Slick, Violent, Nasty and, Maybe Hopeful." *New York Times*, June 17, 1990, Section 4, p. 1.

Parsons, Christi. "U. of C. Law Faculty Didn't Back Kagan: No Job Offer When She Sought Return After Clinton Duty." *Chicago Tribune*, May 30, 2010, http://articles.chicagotribune.com/2010–05–30/news/ct-met-kagan-chicago-20100530_1_harvard-law-school-elena-kagan-faculty.

Peppers, Todd C., and Artemus Ward, eds. *In Chambers: Stories of Supreme Court Law Clerks and Their Justices*. Charlottesville: University of Virginia Press, 2012, p. 315.

"Philadelphia High School for Girls," n.d., http://webgui.phila.k12 .pa.us/schools/g/girlshigh.

Podhoretz, John. "The Upper West Side, Then and Now." *Commentary Magazine*, May 2010, http://www.commentarymagazine.com/article/ the-upper-west-side-then-and-now/.

Princeton University. "Princeton University at a Glance." http://www .princeton.edu/main/about/history/glance/.

Richey, Warren. "Elena Kagan Confirmed to Supreme Court." *CSMonitor*, August 5, 2010, http://www.csmonitor.com/USA/Politics/ 2010/0805/Elena-Kagan-confirmed-to-Supreme-Court.

Ross, Lee. "Kagan in Limited Role as Court Convenes to Tackle Immigration and More." *FoxNews*, October 1, 2010, http://www .foxnews.com/politics/2010/10/01/supreme-court-returns-tackle- immigration-kagan-joins-time/#ixzz2XpTRPCML.

Rudman, Chelsea. "Brietbart Exclusive: Kagan's Notes on Derrick Bell's Law Review Article Were 'Handwritten.'" *Media Matters for America*, April 26, 2012, http://mediamatters.org/blog/2012/04/26/bre itbart-exclusive-kagans-notes-on-derrick-bel/185593.

Saltzman, Jonathan, and Tracy Jan. "At Harvard, Dean Eased Faculty Strife." *Boston Globe*, May 11, 2010, http://www.boston.com/news/ education/higher/articles/2010/05/11/at_harvard_dean_eased_ faculty_strife/.

Savage, Charlie, and Lisa Faye Petak. "A B-Minus? The Shock! The Horror!." *New York Times*, May 24, 2010, http://www.nytimes .com/2010/05/25/us/politics/25kagan.html?_r=0.

Savage, Charlie, and Lisa Faye Petak. "Kagan's Link to Marshall Cuts 2 Ways." *New York Times*, May 12, 2010, http://www.nytimes .com/2010/05/13/us/politics/13marshall.html?pagewanted=all.

Savage, Charlie, and Lisa Faye Petak. "In Supreme Court Work, Early Views of Kagan." *New York Times*, June 3, 2010, http://www.nytimes .com/2010/06/04/us/politics/04kagan.html?pagewanted=all&_r=0.

Schelling, Ameena. "Reserved Passion: Kagan '81." *Daily Princetonian*, May 3, 2010, 2011, http://www.dailyprincetonian.com/2010/05/ 03/26081/.

Scherer, Michael. "Court Nominee Elena Kagan: Let the Scrutiny Start." *Time*, May 10, 2010, http://www.time.com/time/politics/article/0,8599,1988179,00.html.

Schwartz, John. "In a Mentor, Kagan's Critics See Liberal Agenda." *New York Times*, June 25, 2010, http://www.nytimes.com/2010/06/26/us/politics/26mikva.html.

"A Selection of Kagan's Marshall Memos." *New York Times*, June 3, 2010, http://documents.nytimes.com/a-selection-of-kagans-marshall-memos#document/p1.

Smith, Andre. "Tenants' Lawyer Kagan Found Banking on Co-op Success." *Heights and Valley News*, July-August 1981, pp. 1, 11.

Stevens, John Paul. "Resignation Letter." *CSPAN*, n.d., http://www.c-span.org/pdf/stevens040910.pdf.

Stevens, John Paul. "Kagan to Pay $2000 for Excess Collections: Fired by Tenants for Co-op Speculation." *Heights and Valley News*, October, 1981, p. 4.

Stolberg, Sheryl Kay, Katharine Q. Seelye, and Lisa W. Foderaro. "A Climb Marked by Confidence and Canniness." *New York Times*, May 10, 2012, http://www.nytimes.com/2010/05/10/us/politics/10kagan.html?pagewanted=5&_r=0.

Stolberg, Sheryl Kay, Katherine Q. Seelye, and Lisa W. Foderaro. "Pragmatic New Yorker Chose A Careful Path to Washington." *New York Times*, May 11, 2010, Section A, p. 1.

Stolberg, Sheryl Kay. "Stevens's Retirement Is Political Test for Obama." *New York Times*, April 9, 2010, http://www.nytimes.com/2010/04/10/us/politics/10stevens.html.

Stolberg, Sheryl Kay. "At Harvard, Kagan Aimed Sights Higher." *New York Times*, May 25, 2010, http://www.nytimes.com/2010/05/26/us/politics/26kagan.html?pagewanted=all&_r=0.

Stolberg, Sheryl Kay. "Glimpses of Kagan's Views in White House." *New York Times*, June 4, 2012, http://www.nytimes.com/2010/06/05/us/politics/05kagan.html?_r=0.

"Stuyvesant Town History." n.d., http://www.chpcny.org/2010/02/stuyvesant-town-history/

Sweet, Lynn. "Elena Kagan's Chicago Ties: Met Obama at U. of C.; Lived in Lincoln Park." *Chicago Sun-Times*, May 11, 2010, http://blogs.suntimes.com/sweet/2010/05/elena_kagans_chicago_ties_met.html.

Teal, Gloria. "The Spark That Lit the Gay Rights Movement, Four Decades Later." Need to Know, June 30, 2010, http://www.pbs.org/wnet/need-to-know/culture/the-spark-that-lit-the-gay-rights-movement-four-decades-later/1873/.

"Thurgood Marshall." Biography.com, http://www.biography.com/people/thurgood-marshall-9400241?page=1.

"Thurgood Marshall's early life." Thurgood Marshall, http://www.thurgoodmarshall.com/interviews/early_life.htm.

Totenberg, Nina. "Solicitor General Kagan Holds Views Close to Her Chest." NPR, December 22, 2009, http://www.npr.org/templates/story/story.php?storyId=121712227.

Totenberg, Nina. "At Harvard, Kagan Won More Fans than Foes." NPR, n.d., http://www.npr.org/templates/story/story.php?storyId=126826571.

Totenberg, Nina. "Seen As Rising Star, Kagan Has Limited Paper Trail." NPR, n.d., http://www.npr.org/templates/story/story.php?storyId=126611113.

Tsoi, Crystal. "Former Chicago Colleagues Call Kagan 'Tough,' 'Non-Ideological.'" Chicago Maroon, May 11, 2010, http://chicagomaroon.com/2010/05/11/obama-taps-former-professor-elena-kagan-for-supreme-court/.

University of Chicago Law School. "History of the Law School." University of Chicago Law School, n.d., http://www.law.uchicago.edu/school/history.

Vicini, James. "Kagan Bucks 40-Year Trend as Court Pick." Reuters News Agency, May 10, 2010, http://www.reuters.com/article/2010/05/10/us-usa-court-kagan-newsmaker-idUSTRE64910220100510.

Walsh, Mark. "Wait Until Law School to Write About the Law, Kagan Tells Grassly." ABA Journal, June 20, 2010, http://www.abajournal.com/news/article/wait_until_law_school_to_write_about_law_kagan_tells_grassley/.

"The Warren Court." The Supreme Court Historical Society., n.d., http://www.supremecourthistory.org/history-of-the-court/history-of-the-court-2/the-warren-court-1953–1969/.

Waskow, Rabbi Arthur O. "Bat Mitzvah," n.d., http://www.myjewishlearning.com/life/Life_Events/BarBat_Mitzvah/History/Bat_Mitzvah.shtml.

Waxman, Sarah. "The History of the Upper West Side," n.d., http://www.ny.com/articles/upperwest.html.

"What's in Supreme Court Nominee Elena Kagan's Clinton-Era White House Memos?" *Daily Caller*, May 11, 2010, http://dailycaller.com/2010/05/11/what%E2%80%99s-in-supreme-court-nominee-elena-kagan%E2%80%99s-clinton-era-white-house-memos/.

"Whitewater Timeline." *Washington Post*, n.d., http://www.washingtonpost.com/wp-srv/politics/special/whitewater/timeline.htm.

Williams, Juan. "Thurgood Marshall: American Revolutionary," n.d., http://www.thurgoodmarshall.com/home.htm.

Worcester College. "History of the College." Worcester College, n.d., http://www.worc.ox.ac.uk/About-Worcester/History-of-the-College.

COURT CASES

Dehaney v. Winnebago County. New York Times, June 3, 2010, http://documents.nytimes.com/a-selection-of-kagans-marshall-memos#document/p4.

Holder v. Humanitarian Law Project. Oyez, n.d., http://www.oyez.org/cases/2000–2009/2009/2008_08_1498.

Lanzaro v. Monmouth County Correctional Institution Inmates. New York Times, June 3, 2010, http://documents.nytimes.com/a-selection-of-kagans-marshall-memos#document/p10.

Ledbetter v. Taylor. New York Times, June 3, 2010, http://documents.nytimes.com/a-selection-of-kagans-marshall-memos#document/p9.

Paskins v. Illinois. New York Times, June 3, 2010, http://documents.nytimes.com/a-selection-of-kagans-marshall-memos#document/p10.

Salazar v. Buono. Oyez, n.d., http://www.oyez.org/cases/2000–2009/2009/2009_08_472.

Sandidge v. the United States. New York Times, June 3, 2010, http://documents.nytimes.com/a-selection-of-kagans-marshall-memos#document/p4.

Torres v. Oakland Scavenger (1987), http://caselaw.lp.findlaw.com/cgi-bin/
    getcase.pl?court=us&vol=487&invol=312.

"*United States v. Comstock.*" *Oyez*, n.d., http://www.oyez.org/cases/
    2000–2009/2009/2009_08_1224.

United States v. Shonde, 803F. 2d 937 Court of Appeals 8th Circuit,
    1986, http://scholar.google.com/scholar_case?case=3472359426
    723034640&hl=en&as_sdt=2&as_vis=1&oi=scholarr.

INDEX

About the Author

MEG GREENE is a historian and writer living in North Carolina. Her published works include ABC-CLIO's biographies of Henry Louis Gates, Jr., Sonia Sotomayor, and Jane Goodall. Ms. Greene holds advanced degrees in history from the University of Nebraska at Omaha and in historic preservation from the University of Vermont.